# HOW DOES GOD CHANGE US?

## Union

A book series edited by Michael Reeves

*Rejoice and Tremble: The Surprising Good News of the Fear of the Lord*, Michael Reeves (2021)

*What Does It Mean to Fear the Lord?*, Michael Reeves (2021, concise version of *Rejoice and Tremble*)

*Deeper: Real Change for Real Sinners*, Dane C. Ortlund (2021)

*How Does God Change Us?*, Dane C. Ortlund (2021, concise version of *Deeper*)

"This lovely, easy-to-read primer by Dane Ortlund grounds our discipleship in the glowing center of Christianity—our Lord Jesus. It's easy to think that as we grow as Christians, we move on to 'higher things' (whatever that means!), when in fact we simply need to learn the beauty and depth of Jesus and all that he's done for us. That's what Ortlund helps us do here. This book will bless you!"

**Paul E. Miller,** author, *A Praying Life* and *J-Curve: Dying and Rising with Jesus in Everyday Life*

"That angst in your soul for more is a part of the growing process—a gift of hunger and thirst that Jesus, the inexhaustible well, will fill. In *How Does God Change Us?*, Dane Ortlund reminds us that the angst is satisfied not by behavioral modification or some quick fix but by the beauty of friendship with Jesus and the peace more deeply accepted in our souls. If you are hungry and thirsty for more life, more joy, more peace, and more Jesus, this is a book for you."

**Matt Chandler,** Lead Pastor, The Village Church, Dallas, Texas; President, Acts 29 Church Planting Network; author, *The Mingling of Souls* and *The Explicit Gospel*

"Jesus said that our greatest 'work' is to believe. As much as any living author, Dane Ortlund has helped me to believe again by reacquainting me with the stunning tenderness and beauty of Jesus. As I read his words, I can sense my heart growing in trust, devotion, and godly affections, grounded in the Savior's love for me. In this incredibly helpful, pastoral book, Dane works out the implications of that vision of Jesus for personal growth, showing us how the key to going further with Jesus is going deeper in his finished work."

**J. D. Greear,** Lead Pastor, The Summit Church, Raleigh-Durham, North Carolina

"How does God change us as his beloved daughters and sons? Think less of climbing a mountain and more of swimming in a deep ocean of the always-more-ness of Jesus. If you've ever wondered what the Bible really means by 'fixing our gaze on Jesus, the author and perfecter of our faith,' this should be the next book you spend time with. Dane helps us understand that the gospel is more of a person to adore and know than theological propositions and categories to master."

**Scotty Smith,** Pastor Emeritus, Christ Community Church, Franklin, Tennessee; Teacher in Residence, West End Community Church, Nashville, Tennessee

# HOW
# DOES GOD
# CHANGE US?

*DANE C. ORTLUND*

WHEATON, ILLINOIS

*How Does God Change Us?*

Copyright © 2021 by Dane C. Ortlund

Published by Crossway
        1300 Crescent Street
        Wheaton, Illinois 60187

Cover design: Jordan Singer

Cover image: Museum Purchase, Gallery Fund / Bridgeman Images

First printing 2021

Printed in the United States of America

Scripture quotations are from the ESV® Bible (The Holy Bible, English Standard Version®), copyright © 2001 by Crossway, a publishing ministry of Good News Publishers. Used by permission. All rights reserved.

Trade paperback ISBN: 978-1-4335-7403-0
ePub ISBN: 978-1-4335-7405-4
PDF ISBN: 978-1-4335-7404-7
Mobipocket ISBN: 978-1-4335-7406-1

---

**Library of Congress Cataloging-in-Publication Data**

Names: Ortlund, Dane Calvin, author.
Title: How does God change us? / Dane C. Ortlund.
Description: Wheaton, Illinois : Crossway, [2021] | Series: Union | Includes bibliographical references and index.
Identifiers: LCCN 2021002413 (print) | LCCN 2021002414 (ebook) | ISBN 9781433574030 (trade paperback) | ISBN 9781433574047 (epdf) | ISBN 9781433574061 (mobi) | ISBN 9781433574054 (epub)
Subjects: LCSH: Change (Psychology)—Religious aspects—Christianity. | Habit breaking—Religious aspects—Christianity. | Sin—Christianity.
Classification: LCC BV4599.5.C44 O78 2021 (print) | LCC BV4599.5.C44 (ebook) | DDC 233—dc23
LC record available at https://lccn.loc.gov/2021002413
LC ebook record available at https://lccn.loc.gov/2021002414

---

Crossway is a publishing ministry of Good News Publishers.

| VP | | 30 | 29 | 28 | 27 | 26 | 25 | 24 | 23 | 22 | 21 |
|----|----|----|----|----|----|----|----|----|----|----|----|
| 15 | 14 | 13 | 12 | 11 | 10 | 9 | 8 | 7 | 6 | 5 | 4 | 3 | 2 | 1 |

*Affectionately dedicated to*
*the faculty of Covenant Theological Seminary, 2002–2006,*
*who taught me about real change from the Bible,*
*then showed me with their lives*

"Aslan," said Lucy, "you're bigger."

"That is because you are older, little one," answered he.

"Not because you are?"

"I am not. But every year you grow, you will find me bigger."

C. S. LEWIS, *Prince Caspian*

# Contents

# Series Preface

OUR INNER CONVICTIONS AND VALUES shape our lives and our ministries. And at Union—the cooperative ministries of Union School of Theology, Union Publishing, Union Research, and Union Mission (visit www.theolo.gy)—we long to grow and support men and women who will delight in God, grow in Christ, serve the church, and bless the world. This Union series of books is an attempt to express and share those values.

They are values that flow from the beauty and grace of God. The living God is so glorious and kind, he cannot be known without being adored. Those who truly know him will love him, and without that heartfelt delight in God, we are nothing but hollow hypocrites. That adoration of God necessarily works itself out in a desire to grow in Christlikeness. It also fuels a love for Christ's precious bride, the church, and a desire

humbly to serve—rather than use—her. And, lastly, loving God brings us to share his concerns, especially to see his life-giving glory fill the earth.

Each exploration of a subject in the Union series will appear in two versions: a full volume and a concise one. The concise treatments, such as this one, are like shorter guided tours: they stick to the main streets and move on fast. You may find, at the end of this little book, that you have questions or want to explore some more: in that case, the fuller volume will take you further up and further in.

My hope and prayer is that these books will bless you and your church as you develop a deeper delight in God that overflows in joyful integrity, humility, Christlikeness, love for the church, and a passion to make disciples of all nations.

*Michael Reeves*
SERIES EDITOR

# Introduction

THE BIBLE SAYS, "GROW in the grace and knowledge of our Lord and Savior Jesus Christ" (2 Pet. 3:18). But how do we do that? How does God actually change us?

The basic point of this little book is that change is a matter of going deeper. Some believers think change happens through outward improvement—behaving more and more in accord with some moral norm (the biblical law, or the commands of Jesus, or conscience, or whatever). Others think change happens mainly through intellectual addition—understanding doctrine with greater breadth and precision. Others think it comes centrally through felt experience—sensory increase as we worship God.

All three of these elements are included in healthy Christian development (and if any is missing, we are out of proportion and will not grow), but real growth transcends them all. Growing in Christ is not centrally improving or adding or experiencing but *deepening*. Implicit in the notion of deepening is that you already have what you need. Christian growth is bringing what you do and say and even feel into line with what, in fact, you already are.

Let me be clear: We're not after behavior modification in this book. I'm not going to talk to you about setting your alarm earlier or cutting carbs. We're not even going to reflect on tithing or church attendance or journaling or small groups or taking the sacraments or reading the Puritans. All of that can be done out of rottenness of heart. We're talking about *real* change. And we're talking about real change for *real sinners*.

A few things right up front.

First, I'm not going to hurry you. No one else should either. We are complicated sinners. Sometimes we take two steps forward and three steps back. We need time. Be patient with yourself. A sense of urgency, yes; but not a sense of hurry. Overnight transformations are the exception, not the norm. Slow change is still real change.

Second, as you begin this book, open your heart to the possibility of real change in your life. One of the devil's great victories is to flood our hearts with a sense of futility. Perhaps his greatest victory in your life is not a sin you are habitually committing but simply a sense of helplessness as to real growth.

Third, this book is written by a fellow patient, not a doctor. It is written to me as much as by me. Out of failure as much as out of success.

1

# Jesus

THIS IS A BOOK about growing in Christ. The first thing to get clear, then, is what Jesus Christ himself is like. Our growth is not independent personal improvement. It is growth *in Christ*. Who then is he?

The temptation for many of us at this point is to assume we pretty much know what Jesus is like. We've been saved by him. We've spent time in the Bible over the years. We've read some books about him. We've told a few others about him.

And yet, if we are honest, we still find our lives riddled with failure and worry and dysfunction and emptiness.

One common reason we fail to leave sin behind is that we have a domesticated view of Jesus. Not an unorthodox view; we are fully orthodox in our Christology. We understand that he came from heaven as the Son of God to live the life we cannot live and die the death we deserve to die. We affirm his glorious resurrection. We confess with the ancient creeds that he is truly God and truly man. We don't have a heterodox view. We have a domesticated view that, for all its doctrinal precision, has downsized the glory of Christ in our hearts.. We have forgotten that the Bible speaks of "the *unsearchable* riches of Christ" (Eph. 3:8).

So we need to begin by getting clear on who this person is in whom we grow. And we start just there—he is a person. Not just a historical figure, but an actual person, alive and well today. He is to be related to. Trusted, spoken to, listened to. Jesus is not a concept. Not an ideal. Not a force. Growing in Christ is a relational, not a formulaic, experience.

In this chapter I want to mention just one truth about Jesus, perhaps the most neglected and also the most vital truth about him if you are to get real traction in growing spiritually: Jesus is tender with us.

### Tender

Jesus Christ is infinitely gentle. He is the most open and accessible, the most peaceful and accommodating person in the universe. He is the most tender, least abrasive person you will ever come across. Infinite strength, infinite meekness. Dazzlingly resplendent; endlessly calm.

If you had only a few words to define who Jesus is, what would you say? In the one place where he himself tells us about his own heart, he says, "I am gentle and lowly in heart" (Matt. 11:29). And remember that the "heart" in biblical terms is not merely our emotions but the innermost animating center of all that we do. Our deepest loves and desires and ambitions pour out of our hearts. And when Jesus opens himself up and tells us of the fountain, the engine, the throbbing core of all that he does, he says that deeper than anything else, he is gentle and lowly. Peer down into the deepest recesses of Jesus Christ and there we find: gentleness and lowliness.

We who know our hearts resist this. We see the ugliness within. We can hardly face ourselves, we feel so inadequate. And Jesus is perfectly holy, the divine Son of God. It is normal and natural, even in our churches, to sense instinctively that he is holding his people at arm's length. This is why we need a Bible. The testimony of the entire Bible, culminating in Matthew 11:29, is that God defies what we instinctively feel by embracing his people in their mess. He finds penitence, distress, need, and lack irresistible.

You don't have to go through security to get to Jesus. You don't have to get in line or take a ticket. No waving for his attention. No raising your voice to make sure he hears you.

In your smallness, he notices you. In your sinfulness, he draws near to you. In your anguish, he is in solidarity with you.

What we must see is not only that Jesus is gentle toward you but that he is positively drawn toward you when you are most sure he doesn't want to be. It's not only that he is not repelled by your fallenness—he finds your need and emptiness and sorrow irresistible. He is not slow to meet you in your need. It's the difference between a teenager's alarm going off on a Monday morning, forcing him to drag himself out of bed, and that same teen springing out of bed on Christmas morning. Just look at the Savior in Matthew, Mark, Luke, and John. With whom does he hang out? What draws forth his tears? What gets him out of bed in the morning? With whom does he eat lunch? The sidelined, the hollowed out, those long out of hope, those who have sent their lives into meltdown.

**The Real Jesus**

The first thing I want to make clear here, early in this book, is that the real Jesus is gentle and lowly in heart. I say the *real* Jesus because we all unwittingly dilute him. We cut him down to what our minds can naturally imagine. But the Bible corrects us, tells us to stop doing that. We can only create a Jesus in our own image—a Jesus of moderate gentleness and mercy—without a Bible. Scripture tears down that diluted Jesus and lets loose the real Christ. And what we find is that his deepest heart is gentle and lowly.

This is a book about how we change. Let me be plain. *You will not change until you get straight who Jesus is, particularly with regard to his surprising tenderness.* And then spend your whole life long going deeper into the gentleness of Jesus. The only alternative to the real Jesus is to get back on the treadmill—the treadmill of doing your best to follow and honor Jesus but believing his mercy and grace to be a stockpile gradually depleted by your failures, and hoping to make it to death before the mountain of mercy runs out. Here is the teaching of the Bible: If you are in Christ, your sins cause that stockpile to grow all the more. Where sins abound, his grace superabounds. It is in your pockets of deepest shame and regret that his heart dwells *and won't leave.*

As you read this book and as you continue to work your way through life, shed once and for all the reduced Jesus and lift your eyes to the real Jesus, the Jesus whose tenderness ever outstrips and embraces your weaknesses, the Christ whose riches are unsearchable. This Christ is one under whose care and instruction you will finally be able to blossom and grow.

2

# Despair

THERE IS A STRANGE though consistent message throughout the Bible. We are told time and again that the way forward will feel like we're going backward.

The Psalms tell us that those whose hearts are breaking and who feel crushed by life are the people God is closest to (Ps. 34:18). Proverbs tells us it is to the low and the destitute that God shows favor (Prov. 3:34). In Isaiah we are surprised to learn that God dwells in two places: way up high, in the glory of heaven, and way down low, with those void of self-confidence and empty of themselves (Isa. 57:15; 66:1–2). Jesus tells us that "unless a grain of wheat falls into the earth and dies, it remains alone; but if it dies, it bears much fruit" (John 12:24).

Why does the Bible do this? Does God want us always feeling bad about ourselves?

Not at all. It is because of God's very desire that we be joyously happy, filled to overflowing with the uproarious cheer of heaven itself, that he says these things. For he is sending us down into honesty and sanity. He wants us to see our sickness so we can run to the doctor. He wants us to get healed.

Fallen human beings enter into joy only through the door of despair. Fullness can be had only through emptiness. That happens decisively at conversion, as we confess our hopelessly sinful predicament for the first time and collapse into the arms of Jesus, and then remains an ongoing rhythm throughout the Christian life. If you are not growing in Christ, one reason may be that you have drifted out of the salutary and healthy discipline of self-despair.

## The Great Prerequisite

If you feel stuck, defeated by old sin patterns, leverage that despair into the healthy sense of self-futility that is the door through which you must pass if you are to get real spiritual traction. Let your emptiness humble you. Let it take you *down*.

We will come to the positive counterparts to this death in chapters ahead. But we cannot circumvent this stage. It is the great prerequisite to everything else. The pattern of the Christian life is not a straight line up to resurrection existence but a curve down into death and thereby up into resurrection existence. And one thing that means is that we go through life with an ever-deepening sense of how reprehensible, in ourselves, we really are. It was toward the *end* of his life that Paul identified himself as the most award-winning sinner he knew (1 Tim. 1:15). The godliest octogenarians I know are those who feel themselves to be more sinful now than at any time before. They have known the pattern of healthy self-despair. Who of us cannot relate to what the pastor and hymn-writer John Newton wrote in a 1776 letter (at age fifty-one): "The life of faith seems so simple and easy in theory, that I can point it out to others in few words; but in practice it is very difficult, and my advances are so slow, that I hardly dare say I get forward at all."[1]

Have you been brought to despair of what you can achieve in your sanctification? If not, have the courage to look yourself squarely in the mirror. Repent. See your profound poverty. Ask the Lord to forgive your arrogance. As you descend down into death, into knowledge of the futility of what inner change you can achieve by your own efforts, it is there, right there, in that dismay and emptiness, *that God lives*. It is there in that desert that he loves to cause the waters to flow and the trees to bloom. Your despair is all he needs to work with. "Only acknowledge your guilt" (Jer. 3:13). What will ruin your growth is if you look the other way, if you deflect the searching gaze of Purity himself, if you cover over your sinfulness and emptiness with smiles and jokes and then go check your mutual funds again, holding at bay what you know in your deepest heart: you are wicked.

If you plunge down only a little into self-despair, you will rise only a little into joyous growth in Christ. Don't just admit your condition is desperately ruinous. Let yourself feel it. Ponder, unhurriedly, how vile, left to yourself, you are.

## Collapse

But as we despair of our own capacities to generate growth—what then?

There is nothing noble about staying in that pit of despair. Healthy despair is an intersection, not a highway; a gateway, not a pathway. We must go there. But we dare not stay there.

The Bible teaches, rather, that each experience of despair is to melt us afresh into deeper fellowship with Jesus. Like jumping on a trampoline, we are to go down into freshly felt emptiness but then let that spring us high into fresh heights with Jesus. The Bible calls this two-step movement repentance and faith.

Repentance is turning from Self. Faith is turning to Jesus. You can't have one without the other. Repentance that does not turn to Jesus is not real repentance; faith that has not first turned from Self is not real faith. If we are traveling the wrong direction, things get fixed as we turn away from the wrong direction and simultaneously begin going the right direction. Both happen together.

Some Christians seem to think that the Christian life is ignited with a decisive act of repentance and then fed by faith thereafter. But as Luther taught, all of life is repentance. The first thesis of his Ninety-Five Theses reads, "When our Lord and Master Jesus Christ said, 'Repent' (Matt. 4:17), he willed the entire life of believers to be one of repentance." The Christian life is one of *repenting our way forward*.

Equally, we live our whole lives by faith. Paul said not "I was converted by faith" but "I live by faith" (Gal. 2:20). We do not merely begin the Christian life by faith; we progress by faith. It is our new normal. We process life, we navigate this mortal existence, by a moment-by-moment turning to God in trust and hope at each juncture, each decision, each passing hour. We "walk by faith, not by sight" (2 Cor. 5:7). That is, we move through life with our eyes looking ever up.

Repentance and faith. In a word: collapse.

Both repentance and faith, however, must never be viewed in isolation from Jesus himself. They are connectors to Christ. They are not "our contribution." They simply are the roads by which we get to real healing: Christ himself.

As you despair of yourself—agonizing over the desolation wrought by your failures, your weaknesses, your inadequacies—let that despair take you way down deep into honesty with yourself. For there you will find a friend, the living Lord Jesus himself, who will startle and surprise you with his gentle goodness as you leave Self behind, in repentance, and bank on him afresh, in faith.

3

# Union

WE HAVE SHARPENED OUR VISION of who Jesus is. And we have established the ongoing salutary reality of self-despair and collapsing in penitent faith time and again into the arms of that Jesus. But does this Jesus remain at a distance? How do we actually access him?

The New Testament gives a resounding answer. Those who collapse into him in repentance and faith are united to him—joined to him—*one* with him. This is the controlling center, according to the New Testament, of what it means to be a Christian. And most fundamentally it is our union with Christ that, according to Scripture, fosters growth (e.g., Rom. 6:1–5).

## Macro and Micro

But what does it mean to be "in" Christ?

The New Testament uses the language of union with Christ in basically two ways. We could call them the macro and the micro realities to union with Christ, or the cosmic and the intimate, or the federal and the personal.

The macro dimension to union with Christ is that he is your leader, and as he goes, so you go. His fate is yours. Why? Because you are *in* him. That may sound a little odd, especially for those of us who live in the West today. But for most human cultures throughout most of human history, including Bible times, this way of thinking about a leader and his people was normal and natural. The formal name for it is "corporate solidarity." If you've ever heard Christ referred to as believers' "federal" head, that's getting at the same notion. The idea is that the one represents the many, and the many are represented by the one.

We see it, for example, in 2 Corinthians 5:14, speaking of the work of Christ and how it connects to us: "One has died for all, therefore all have died." Because Christ died, and those united to him share in his fate, we too have "died" (see also Rom. 6:6, 8).

To be in Christ, then, in this macro or cosmic or federal way, is for our destiny to be bound up with his rather than with Adam's. First Corinthians 15:22 is the whole Bible in a short sentence: "As in Adam all die, so also in Christ shall all be made alive." The alternative to being in Christ is to be in Adam. One or the other. No third option. The most famous athletes, the cultural icons, those whose fans treat them like gods—what is most deeply true of them is that they are either in Adam or in Christ.

But there is a closer, more intimate reality to union with Christ—the micro dimension—and sometimes the biblical authors speak of our union in this way. It is difficult to know exactly how to express it. The Bible uses imagery to communicate it, perhaps because this reality is better likened than defined. We are given images such as a vine and its branches, or a head and the other body parts, or even a groom and his bride. In all cases there is an organic, intimate uniting, a sharing of properties, a oneness. The vine gives life to the branches; the head directs and cares for its body parts; the husband "nourishes and cherishes" his wife as he does his own body (Eph. 5:29; see also 1 Cor. 6:13–18).

Your salvation in the gospel is far deeper, far more wondrous, than walking an aisle or praying a prayer or raising a hand or going forward at an evangelistic rally. Your salvation is to be united to the living Christ himself. In that most intimate of unions, we are given back our true selves. You become the you that you were meant to be. You recover your original destiny. You realize that your existence out of Christ was a shadow of what you were made to be. In other words, it is only in union with Christ that you can grow into who God made you to be.

## Safe and Secure

But how does our union with Christ actually foster growth and change?

How could it *not*? Note the sheer intimacy and safety of being a Christian. Our Christian growth takes place in the sphere of a wonderful inevitability, even invincibility. I am united to Christ. I can never be disunited from him. The logic of the New Testament letters is that in order for me to get disunited from Christ, Christ himself would have to be de-resurrected. He'd have to get kicked out of heaven for me to get kicked out of him. We're that safe.

Think of yourself as an onion. The outer peel consists of peripheral things about you, the parts of you that don't matter much: your clothes, the car you drive, things like that. If you peel away that layer, what's next? A collection of things slightly more essential to who you are: the family you were raised in, your personality profile, your blood type, your volunteer work. Peel that away. The next deeper layer is your relationships: your dearest friends, your roommates if you're a student, your spouse if you're married. Peel that away. The next deeper layer is what you believe about the world, the truths you cherish deep in your heart: who you believe God is, what your final future is, where you think world history is heading. The next deeper layer after that comprises your sins and secrets, past and present, things about you no one else knows.

Keep peeling away layer after layer, everything that makes you *you*. What do you find at the core? You are united to Christ. That is the most irreducible reality about you. Peel everything else away, and the solid, immovable truth about you is your union with a resurrected Christ.

## Taking It Deep

Let your mind and heart go way down deep into the reality of your union with the living Lord Jesus Christ. If you are in him, you have everything you need to grow. By the Holy Spirit, you are in him and he is in you. He is both your federal head and your intimate companion. *You cannot lose.* You are inexhaustibly rich. For you are one with Christ, and he is himself inexhaustibly rich, the heir of the universe.

Submerge yourself in this truth. Let it wash over you. The divine Son, through whom all things were made (Col. 1:16), who "upholds the universe by the word of his power" (Heb. 1:3), is the one with whom you have been united. Through no activity of your own, but by the sheer and mighty grace of God, you have been enveloped in the triumphant and tender ruler of the cosmos.

Therefore: *nothing can touch you that does not touch him.* To get to you, every pain, every assault, every disappointment has to go through him. You are shielded by invincible love. He himself feels your anguish even more deeply than you do, because you're one with him; and he mediates everything hard in your life through his love for you, because you're one with him. Picture yourself standing in a circle with an invisible but impenetrable wall surrounding you, a sphere of impregnability. But it's not a circle you're in. It's a person—*the* person. The one before whom John fell down as he grappled for words to describe what he was looking at as one whose "eyes were like a flame of fire . . . and his voice was like the roar of many waters" (Rev. 1:14–15) has been made one with you. The might of heaven, the power that flung galaxies into existence, has swept you into himself.

And you're there to stay. Amid the storms of your little existence—the sins and sufferings, the failure and faltering, the waywardness and wandering—he is going to walk you right into heaven. He is not just with you. He is in you, and you in him. His destiny now falls on you. His union with you at both the macro and micro levels guarantees your eventual glory and rest and calm. You may as well question gravity as question the certainty of what your union with him means for your final future.

So consider the darkness that remains in your life. Our sins loom large. They seem so insurmountable. But Christ and your union with him loom larger still. As far as sin in your life reaches, Christ and your union with him reach further. As deep as your failure goes, Christ and your union with him go deeper still. Rest in the knowledge that your sins and failures can never kick you out of Christ. Let an ever-deepening awareness of your union with him strengthen your resistance to sin. See it in the Bible. Ponder his tireless care for you. You have been strengthened with the power to fight and overcome sin because the power that raised Jesus from the dead now resides in you, living and active—for Jesus Christ himself resides in you. You can never be justifiably accused ever again. "There is therefore now no condemnation for those who are *in* Christ Jesus" (Rom. 8:1).

Draw strength from your oneness with Jesus. You are no longer alone. No longer isolated. When you sin, don't give up. Let him pick you up and put you on your feet again with fresh dignity. He lifts your chin, looks you in the eye, and defines your existence: "you in me, and I in you" (John 14:20).

4

# Embrace

THE FIRST THREE CHAPTERS have briefly laid a foundation—
Jesus Christ's gentleness (chap. 1), our emptiness (chap. 2), and our
union with him (chap. 3). Now we begin to get into the actual dy-
namics by which believers change. We begin with the love of God.

What is the love of God? To ask that question is the same as
to ask, what is God? The Bible says not simply that "God loves"
but also that "God is love" (1 John 4:8, 16). Love, for the God of
the Bible, is not one activity among others. Love defines who he
is most deeply. Ultimate reality is not cold, blank, endless space.
Ultimate reality is an eternal fountain of endless, unquenchable
love. A love so great and so free that it could not be contained
within the uproarious joy of Father, Son, and Spirit but spilled out
to create and embrace finite and fallen humans into it. Divine love

is inherently spreading, engulfing, embracing, overflowing. If you are a Christian, *God made you so that he could love you.*

What I want to say in this chapter is that the love of God is not something to see once and believe and then move beyond to other truths or strategies for growing in Christ. The love of God is what we feed on our whole lives long, wading ever more deeply into this endless ocean. And that feeding, that wading, is itself what fosters growth. *We grow in Christ no further than we enjoy his embrace of us.* His tender, mighty, irreversible embrace into his own divine heart.

### The Unknowable Love of Christ

Paul didn't pray the tepid prayers we often pray. He prayed God-sized prayers. In one of the most spiritually nuclear passages in all the Bible he prays that his readers "may have strength to comprehend with all the saints what is the breadth and length and height and depth, and to know the love of Christ that surpasses knowledge, that you may be filled with all the fullness of God" (Eph. 3:18–19).

What exactly is Paul praying for? Not for greater obedience among the Ephesians, or that they would be more fruitful, or that false teaching would be stamped out, or that they would grow in doctrinal depth, or even for the spread of the gospel. All good things! But here Paul prays that the Ephesians would be given supernatural power—not power to perform miracles or walk on water or convert their neighbors, but power, such power, the kind that only God himself can give, strength to *know how much Jesus loves them.* Not just to have the love of Christ. To *know* the love of Christ. It's the difference between looking at a postcard of the Hawaii beach and sitting on that beach, blinking, squinting, absorbing the sun's warmth.

What is this love of Christ?

Niceness? Certainly not—this is the Christ who took the time to make a whip and then used it to drive the money changers from the temple, flipping over tables.

Is it a refusal to judge people? By no means: Scripture speaks of his judgment like a sharp two-edged sword coming out of his mouth (Rev. 1:16; 2:12).

The love of Christ is his settled, unflappable heart of affection for sinners and sufferers—and *only* sinners and sufferers. When Jesus loves, Jesus is Jesus. He is being true to his own innermost depths. He doesn't have to work himself up to love. He is a gorged river of love, pent up, ready to gush forth upon the most timid request for it. Love is who Jesus most deeply, most naturally is.

## His Settled Heart, Our Settled Hearts

Your growth in Christ will go no further than your settledness, way down deep in your heart, that God loves you. That he has pulled you in to his own deepest heart. His affection for his own never wanes, never sours, never cools. That thing about you that makes you wince most only strengthens his delight in embracing you. At your point of deepest shame and regret, that's where Christ loves you the most. The old Puritan Thomas Goodwin wrote that "Christ is love covered over with flesh."[1] It's who he is.

Divine love is not calculating and cautious, like ours. The God of the Bible is unrestrained. If we are united to Jesus Christ, our sins do not cause his love to take a hit. Though our sins will make *us* more miserable, they cause his love to surge forward all the more. One day we will stand before him, quietly, unhurriedly, overwhelmed with relief and standing under the felt flood of divine affection in a way we never can here in this life. But in the meantime our lifeline to sustain us in this fallen world is that very love and our heart knowledge of it. Knowing this love is what draws us toward God in this life. We can revere his greatness, but it does not draw us to him; his goodness, his love, draws us in.

## Blockages to Knowing His Love

And yet it often isn't that simple, is it? Some of us, no matter how much we try, no matter how much Bible we read, find the experience of God's love elusive.

Some of us look at the evidence of our lives, mindful of the pain we've endured, and we do not know how to respond except with cold cynicism. *The love of Christ?* we wonder. *Is this a joke?*

*You're living in la-la land, Dane. This all sounds nice in theory. But look at the wreckage of my life. I know deep down in my bones I was created to be a palace, magnificent and stately. But I'm a pile of bombed-out rubble given the way others have treated me, wronged me, victimized me. My life disproves the love of Christ.*

If you are having thoughts like that as you hear of Christ's love, I want you to know that you're looking at the wrong life. *Your* life doesn't *disprove* Christ's love; *his* life *proves* it.

In heaven, the eternal Son of God was "palatial" magnificence if anything ever was. But he became a man and, instead of ruling in glorious authority as one would expect of God-become-man, he was rejected and killed. His own life was reduced to bombed-out rubble. Why? So that he could sweep sinful you into his deepest heart and never let you go, having satisfied the Father's righteous wrath toward you in his atoning death.

Your suffering does not define you. His does. You have endured pain involuntarily. He has endured pain voluntarily, for you. Your pain is meant to push you to flee to him, where he endured what you deserve.

If Jesus himself was willing to journey down into the suffering of hell, you can bank everything on his love as you journey through your own suffering on your way up to heaven.

For others of you, it isn't so much what you have received at the hands of others but your own sin and folly that cause you to doubt God's love. You are a follower of Jesus and you keep messing up. You wonder when the reservoir of divine love is going to run dry.

Here's what I say to you: Do you realize how God treats his children who stiff-arm his love?

He loves them all the fiercer.

It's who he is. He is love. He is a fountain of affection. He is tireless, unquitting, in his embrace. Let him love you all over again. Pick yourself up off the ground, stop feeling sorry for yourself, and allow his heart to plunge you into his oceanic love more deeply than he ever has before.

Whether the wreckage of your life is your own doing or someone else's, you who are in Christ have never stepped outside the cascading waterfall of divine love. God would have to un-God himself for that deluge to run dry. You have muted your experience of his love. But you cannot stop the flow any more than a single pebble can slow Victoria Falls, a mile across and 360 feet high, as those millions of gallons of the Zambezi River come crashing over the cliffs there in southern Zambia.

Whether you have ignored it, neglected it, squandered it, misunderstood it, or hardened yourself to it—the Lord Jesus Christ approaches you today not with arms crossed but with arms open, the very position in which he hung on the cross, and he says to you:

*None of that matters right now. Don't give it another thought.*

*All that matters now is you and me.*

*You know you are a mess. You are a sinner. Your entire existence has been built around you.*

*Step in out of that storm. Let your heart crack open to Joy.*

*I was punished so that you don't have to be. I was arrested so you could go free. I was indicted so you could be exonerated. I was executed so you could be acquitted.*

*And all of that is just the beginning of my love. That proved my love, but it's not an endpoint; it's only the doorway into my love.*

*Humble yourself enough to receive it.*

*Plunge your parched soul into the sea of my love. There you will find the rest and relief and embrace and friendship your heart longs for.*

The wraparound category of your life is not your performance but God's love. The defining hallmark of your life is not your cleanness but his embrace. The deepest destiny of your life is to descend ever deeper, with quiet yet ever-increasing intensity, into the endless love of God. We grow spiritually by getting a head start on that project, right here in this fallen earthly life.

5

# Acquittal

WE GROW IN CHRIST as we go deeper into, rather than moving on from, the verdict of acquittal that got us into Christ in the first place.

The gospel is not a hotel to pass through but a home to live in. Not jumper cables to get the Christian life started but an engine to keep the Christian life going.

Think of it this way: This is a book about sanctification. How do we move forward spiritually? And in this book on sanctification, this chapter is on justification. Sanctification is lifelong, gradual growth in grace. Justification, however, is not a process but an event, a moment in time, the verdict of legal acquittal once and for all. Why then are we thinking about justification in a book about sanctification? Here's why: *the process of sanctification is, in large part, fed by constant returning, ever more deeply, to the event of justification.*

But let's be more specific, bearing in mind that growth in Christ is a matter of transformation from the inside out, as opposed to merely externally oriented behavioral conformity. We could put the point of this chapter in three sentences:

1. Justification is outside-in, and we lose it if we make it inside-out.
2. Sanctification is inside-out, and we lose it if we make it outside-in.
3. And this inside-out sanctification is largely fed by daily appropriation of this outside-in justification.

### Justification and Sanctification

First, justification is outside-in, and we lose it if we make it inside-out. In other words, justification is "outside-in" in the sense that we are justified by being given a right standing that comes to us from wholly outside us. This is strange and difficult to get our minds around at first. The very notion of a person's standing, an assessment of whether someone is guilty or innocent, universally depends on his or her own performance. Yet in the gospel we are given what the Reformers called an "alien righteousness" because the record of Jesus is given to us. In what

Luther called the "happy exchange," we are given Christ's righteous record and he takes on our sin-ridden record; accordingly, we are treated as innocent and Christ was treated as guilty, bearing our punishment on the cross. We are thus "justified"—that is, declared faultless with respect to our legal standing.

We resist this. Way down deep, we try to strengthen God's verdict over our lives through our own subtle contributions. But to do this is to turn justification from an outside-in truth to an inside-out truth. We lose entirely the comfort of justification if it is vulnerable to any self-strengthening. It must be all or nothing.

Sanctification, on the other hand, is inside-out, and we lose it if we make it outside-in.

Our growth in godliness, in other words, works in an inverse way to justification, both in how it works and in how it gets ruined. In our justification the verdict of legal acquittal must come wholly from heaven, landing on us as something earned by someone outside us, in no way helped out by our contribution. But that has to do with our *standing*. Sanctification, however, is change with regard to our *walk*, our personal holiness, the subjective result of the gospel. This must happen internally.

And just as we ruin the comfort of justification if we make it internal, we ruin the reality of sanctification if we make it external. But growth in godliness is not generated by conformity to any external code—whether the Ten Commandments or the commands of Jesus or self-imposed rules or your own conscience. This does not mean the commands of Scripture are worthless. On the contrary, they are "holy and righteous and good" (Rom. 7:12). But the commands of the Bible are the steering wheel, not the engine, to your growth. They are vitally instructive, but they do not themselves give you the power you need to obey the instruction.

### Sanctification by Justification

And inside-out sanctification is largely fed by daily appropriation of outside-in justification.

The outside-in verdict nurtures the inside-out process. You can't crowbar your way into change. You can only be melted. Reflection on the wonder of the gospel—that we are justified simply by looking away from self to the finished work of Christ on our behalf—softens our hearts. The labor of sanctification becomes wonderfully calmed. The gospel is what changes us, and only it can, because the gospel itself is telling us what is true of us before we ever begin to change, and no matter how slowly our change comes.

We intuitively think that the way to grow is to hear exhortation. And exhortation has an important place. We are not mature Christians if we can never bear to hear the challenges and commands of Scripture. But the Bible teaches that healthy spiritual growth takes place only when such commands land on those who know they are accepted and safe irrespective of the degree to which they successfully keep those commands.

This need to return constantly to the freeness of the doctrine of justification must be emphasized because the fall rewires us to do precisely the opposite. Our fallen hearts are spring-loaded to assess our justified state on the basis of how our sanctification is going. But we grow in Christ by placing our sanctification in the light of our justification. The old English pastor Thomas Adam reflected on this truth in his diary, calling it "sanctification by justification." He wrote: "Justification by sanctification is man's way to heaven. . . . Sanctification by justification is God's."[1] In his classic work on union with Christ, James Stewart wrote: "It is God's justifying verdict itself which sanctifies. . . . It is precisely because God waits for no guarantees but pardons out-and-out . . . that forgiveness regenerates, and justification sanctifies."[2] Dutch theologian G. C. Berkouwer argues repeatedly throughout his study of sanctification that "the heart of sanctification is the life which feeds on . . . justification."[3]

## Real Approval

Let's make this real practical.

Perhaps you believe in justification by faith but still find yourself lapsing back into, say, the need for approval from other people. Consider this: the most famous statement in all the Bible on justification by faith—Galatians 2:16—is brought to bear on the very same problem. Paul gives a teaching on justification not to unbelievers but to believers—indeed, to a fellow apostle, Peter himself. Why? Because Peter was "fearing" the circumcision party (Gal. 2:12). Peter had not settled in his heart what Paul had: "Am I now seeking the approval of man, or of God? Or am I trying to please man?" (Gal. 1:10). Paul identifies Peter's conduct as being out of step with the gospel (Gal. 2:14) and in violation of the doctrine of justification by faith (Gal. 2:16) because *Peter allowed the approval of people to erode his grasp of the approval that the gospel gives and the settled status that justification provides.*

At conversion we understand the gospel for the first time, and we feel the immense relief of being forgiven of our sins and granted a new status in the family of God. We learn for the first time that we are legally acquitted, innocent, free to leave the courtroom. But even for Christians, there remain regions within that continue to resist the grace of the gospel without our even realizing it. And one vital aspect of growing in Christ is coming back time and again to the doctrine of justification to do chemotherapy on the remaining malignancies of our craving for human approval.

Live your life out of the fullness of a justified existence. Let Jesus Christ clothe you, dignify you, justify you. Nothing else can.

Do you want to grow in Christ? Never graduate beyond the gospel. Move ever deeper into the gospel. The freeness of your outside-in justification is a critical ingredient to fostering your inside-out sanctification.

6

# Honesty

TO THIS POINT we have been reflecting on what happens between God and me in fostering growth. But to these vertical realities we must join the horizontal. A Christian is connected not only *up*, to God, but also *out*, to other Christians. Scripture calls believers the body of Christ. We live our lives in Christ in a way that is vitally, organically joined to all other believers. We who are in Christ are no more detached from other believers than muscle tissue can be detached from ligaments in a healthy body.

The Bible has much to say about how we are to interact with each other as fellow Christians if we are to grow. I'd like to focus in this chapter on one particularly important teaching from the New Testament, the most important corporate reality for our growth in Christ: honesty.

## Walking in the Light

The Bible says, "If we walk in the light, as he is in the light, we have fellowship with one another, and the blood of Jesus his Son cleanses us from all sin" (1 John 1:7). As the surrounding context makes clear, "walking in the light" in this text is not living in moral purity but rather *honesty with other Christians*. And what we must realize, if we are to grow in Christ, is that we are restricting our growth if we do not move through life doing the painful, humiliating, liberating work of cheerfully bringing our failures out from the darkness of secrecy into the light of acknowledgment before a Christian brother or sister. In the darkness, our sins fester and grow in strength. In the light, they wither and die. Walking in the light, in other words, is honesty with God and others.

We consign ourselves to plateaued growth in Christ if we yield to pride and fear and hide our sins. We grow as we own up to being real sinners, not theoretical sinners. All of us, as Christians, acknowledge generally that we are sinners. Rarer is the Christian who opens up to another about exactly *how* he or she is a sinner. But in this honesty, life blossoms.

Walking in the light is killing the preening and parading, the mask-wearing, the veneer, the keeping up of appearances. It is collapsing into transparency.

Everything in us resists this. Sometimes it feels like we would rather die. Actually, walking in the light is a certain kind of death. It feels as if our whole personhood, our self, is going into meltdown. We are losing our impressive appearance in front of another Christian. But what would you say to a baby terrified of being born, wanting to stay in the warmth and darkness of the womb, refusing to come out into the light? You would say: *If you stay in there, you will die. The way into life and growth is to come out into the light.*

Here's what happens when we begin to get honest, even with just one other person. The two circles of what we know ourselves to be and what we present ourselves to be overlap. Rather than the private Dane being one person and the public Dane a different person, there's just one Dane. We become whole. Integrated. Strong. But the keeping up of appearances is an exhausting way to live.

Honesty with each other has many powerful results. This verse mentions two:

1. We have fellowship with one another.
2. The blood of Jesus his Son cleanses us from all sin.

We'll take them in that order.

## Fellowship with One Another

We were made to be together, to speak to each other, to share our hearts, to laugh together, to co-enjoy a beautiful flower.

The pain of a sorrow is doubled when endured alone but greatly lessened when borne by another alongside us; likewise the satisfaction of a joy is doubled when celebrated with another yet lessened when enjoyed alone. We pant for a bonded spirit with others, for shared hearts, for togetherness. Often our idolatrous pursuits through sexual immorality, overindulgence in alcohol, or social media platform-building are all simply misplaced longings for human fellowship. If we traced those heart-eroding pursuits down to their source, we would find, among other things, simply an absence of real Christian fellowship.

As we walk in the light with each other, the walls come crashing down. We relax into a new way of being, a liberated way of existing with one another. Fellowship ignites and burns brightly. We are actually able to enjoy others, instead of just using them or constantly being in impress mode. Indeed, keeping up appearances has become so normal to us, we don't even realize how deeply we're mired in it. Surely one of the shocks of the new earth, when all our fallenness and sin and self-concern has evaporated, will be the startling new freedom and pleasure of simply being around other people. Emptied of any need to present ourselves a certain way, we will have finally come truly alive. We will be free.

The message of the New Testament is that we can begin to enjoy that freedom—not perfectly, but truly—now. Which brings us to the second result of walking in the light.

## Cleansing from All Sin

"The blood of Jesus his Son cleanses us from all sin." This little statement tucked into the back end of 1 John 1:7 is the whole reason any one of us will ever make it to heaven one day. We are cleansed by the blood of Christ. We are given a bath. A one-time, permanently effective, cascading cleansing.

We'll keep sinning in lots of ways, of course, but what is most deeply true of us is that we have been decisively washed clean once and for all. In culminating fulfillment of the shed blood of the Passover lamb in the Old Testament law, Jesus stood in for his people and let his own blood be taken on their behalf. He offered his own life so that all who desire for Jesus's blood to stand in for the taking of their own blood can have that substitutionary transaction determine their own eternal destiny. In that way his blood cleanses us. Jesus, the clean one, was treated as dirty so that I, the dirty one, am treated as clean.

Many of us feel irredeemably dirty. We know God loves us, and we believe we really are justified. But in the meantime we can't get out from under the oppressive sense of dirtiness. *The gospel answers that.* If you are in Christ, heaven has bathed you. You have been rinsed clean and are now "un-dirty-able." Jesus was defiled to free you from your defiled status and your defiled feelings.

A thoughtful reader may respond at this point: *The text says that "if we walk in the light . . . the blood of Jesus his Son cleanses us from all sin." Does that mean if we're not honest with each other, God won't cleanse us?*

We know from the broader teaching of the Bible that this is not so. The text means that as we walk in the light, the cleansing blood of Christ becomes more real to us. It moves from believed theory to felt reality. We experience that forgiveness more deeply than we otherwise can. Our hearts crack open to receive it more deeply than before. When you trust God enough to speak your sinfulness to another human, the channels of your heart are opened to feeling forgiven. This is because the same pride that stops us from confessing our sins to a brother or sister also hinders our felt belief in the gospel. Evading honesty before another Christian is more fundamentally a rejection of the gospel itself. Refusing to be honest with another is works righteousness in disguise; we are believing that we need to save face, retain uprightness of appearance. This is why confessing our sins to another naturally makes the gospel itself more real to us.

### Collapse into Flourishing

Do you want joy? John did say, after all, that he was writing 1 John "so that our joy may be complete" (1:4). Do you want to grow? Perhaps just on the other side of real honesty with another Christian there awaits you a depth of "fellowship . . . with the Father and with his Son Jesus Christ" (1:3) that will make what you presently believe seem, in comparison, utterly unreal.

Believe the gospel. Find a trustworthy friend. Bring that brother or sister into your fallenness in a redemptive but humiliatingly transparent way. Humble yourself down into the death of honesty and see what life blossoms on the other side. Find yourself feeling bathed afresh in the gospel of grace. And as you dare to go deeper into honesty and deeper into the experience of the cleansing blood of Christ, watch your heart relax into the growth you long for.

7

# Pain

MISERY AND DARKNESS AND ANGUISH and regret and shame and lament color all that we say, do, and think. The reality of nightmares shows that this pain and futility even reaches into our subconscious and our sleep. We can go *nowhere* to escape the futility and pain of life in this fallen world. Pain is not the islands of our life but the ocean; disappointment and let-down is the stage on which all of life unfolds, not an occasional blip on an otherwise comfortable and smooth life.

And a crucial building block in our growth in grace is a humble openness to receiving the bitternesses of life as God's gentle way of drawing us out of the misery of self and more deeply into spiritual maturity. Through pain God is inviting us up into "mature manhood, to the measure of the stature of the fullness of Christ" (Eph. 4:13; see also Rom. 8:17).

## Slicing Off Branches

Each of us is like an otherwise healthy vine that has the perverse inclination to entangle all its tendrils around a poisonous tree that appears nourishing but actually deadens us. We have been told that touching this tree will kill us. But we can't help ourselves. We wrap ourselves around it. There's only one resort for the loving gardener. He must slice us free. Lop off whole branches, even.

The world and its fraudulent offerings are like that poisonous tree. The biblical category for this perverse inclination of our hearts to look to the things of this world to quench our soul thirst is *idolatry*. Idolatry is the folly of asking a gift to be a giver. The Bible tells us instead to locate our supreme longings and thirstings in God himself. He alone can satisfy (Ps. 16:11), and he promises he will satisfy (Jer. 31:25). And our heavenly Gardener loves us too much to let us continue to commit soul suicide by getting more and more deeply attached to the world. Through the pain of disappointment and frustration, God weans us from the love of this world.

When life hurts, we immediately find ourselves at an internal fork in the road. Either we take the road of cynicism, withdrawing from openheartedness with God and others, retreating into the felt safety of holding back our desires and longings, lest they get hurt again, or we press into greater depth with God than we have ever known. Either we smirk at what we said we believed about God's sovereignty and goodness, thinking that pain has just disproven what we said we believed, or we put even more weight on our theology. The two circles of professed theology and heart theology, to that point distinct, are forced either to move farther away than ever or to perfectly overlap. Either we let the divine physician continue the operation, or we insist on being wheeled out of the operating room. But pain does not let us go on as before.

If you want to be a solid, weighty, radiant old man or woman someday, let the pain in your life force you to believe your own theology. Let it propel you into deeper fellowship with Christ than ever before. Don't let your heart dry up. He is in your pain. He is refining you. All that you will lose is the Self and misery that in your deepest heart you want to shed anyway. God loves us too much to let us remain shallow.

Your tears are his tools.

## Mortification

Alongside the kind of pain in which we are passive is another kind of pain in which we are active. I refer to the age-old discipline that theologians call mortification.

*Mortification* is just a theological word for "putting to death." It refers to the duty of every Christian to kill sin. As John Owen put it in the most important work ever written on killing sin, "Be killing sin or sin will be killing you."[1] None of us is ever in neutral. Right now, every one of us who is in Christ is either killing sin or being killed by sin. Either getting stronger or getting weaker. If you think you're coasting, you're actually going backward. It may feel as if you're currently in neutral, but our hearts are like gardens: if we aren't proactively rooting out the weeds, the weeds are growing.

Mortification is the most *active* facet of our growing in Christ. The verse on which John Owen based his book on mortification was Romans 8:13: "For if you live according to the flesh you will die, but if by the Spirit you put to death [i.e., mortify] the deeds of the body, you will live." As we find ourselves being pulled down by sin and temptation, we cry out to the Spirit for grace and help, and then we act in conscious dependence on that Spirit, taking it by faith that we are, thanks to the Spirit, able to kill that sin or resist that temptation. The devil wants us to think we are impotent. But if God the Spirit is within us, the very power that raised Jesus's dead body to triumphant life is able to exert that same vital power in our little lives (Rom. 8:11).

In speaking of pain as a vital ingredient to our growth, and especially now as we speak of our self-inflicted "pain" of mortification, we must be careful not to view the pain of our lives as in any way contributing to Christ's atoning work. That may sound obvious, but the temptation to do so is subtle and insidious. We must remember what we rehearsed in chapter 5 about acquittal. In the finished work of Christ on the cross we are completely liberated from the accusing powers of the devil and our own consciences. In killing sin we are not completing Christ's finished work; we are responding to it. Christ was killed so that our own relative success or failure in killing sin is no part of the formula of our adoption into God's family.

## Suffocating Sin

How, practically, do we mortify sin?

We don't mainly kill sin by looking at it. We have to be aware of it, of course. But we don't kill sin the way a soldier kills an enemy in battle, by zeroing in on the enemy himself. Killing sin is a strange battle because it happens by *looking away from the sin*. By "looking away" I don't mean emptying our minds and trying to create a mental vacuum. I mean looking at Jesus Christ. In the same way that playing matchbox cars on the front lawn loses its attractiveness when we're invited to spend the afternoon at a NASCAR race, sin loses its appeal as we allow ourselves to be re-enchanted time and again with the unsurpassable beauty of Jesus.

We feed sin by coddling it, pining after it, daydreaming about it, giving vent to it. We suffocate sin by redirecting our gaze to Christ. As our hearts redirect their gaze to the Jesus of the Bible in all his glorious gentleness and dazzling love, sin gets starved and begins to wilt. As we enjoy the truths this book has been reflecting on—realities such as our union with Christ and his unshakable embrace of us and God's irreversible acquittal of us—then, right then, spiritual life and vigor begin to have the ascendancy, and the grip of sin loosens.

There is no special technique to mortifying sin. You simply open your Bible and unleash it, letting God surprise you each day with the wonder of his love, proven in Christ and experienced in the Spirit.

**Fighting Is Winning**

Are you struggling with sin today? The struggle itself reflects life. If we were not regenerate, we simply wouldn't care. The longing for Christ, the frustration at our falls, the desire to be fully yielded to God—these are the cries of life, even if immature life. God will not let you go. He will be sure to love you on into heaven.

In the meantime, he is teaching you not to give up your mortification project. Your very efforts to fight your sin distress

Satan. Fighting is winning. C. S. Lewis put it well in a January 1942 letter, and with this word of comfort we close this chapter:

> I know all about the despair of overcoming chronic temptations.
>
> It is not serious provided self-offended petulance, annoyance at breaking records, impatience etc doesn't get the upper hand. *No amount* of falls will really undo us if we keep on picking ourselves up each time. We shall of course be very muddy and tattered children by the time we reach home. But the bathrooms are all ready, the towels put out, and the clean clothes are airing in the cupboard.
>
> The only fatal thing is to lose one's temper and give it up. It is when we notice the dirt that God is most present to us: it is the very sign of His presence.[2]

8

# Breathing

ALL THE CHAPTERS OF THIS BOOK till now have reflected on overarching themes. Realities such as union with Christ, or the embrace of Christ, or acquittal before God through the wonder of justification—these are timeless truths we spend a lifetime believing and absorbing into our hearts. But how, practically, day by day, do we do that? What are the actual tools by which that belief and heart absorption take place?

This chapter answers that question. In truth there are many valid answers to the question—the sacraments of the church, Christian fellowship, good books, and so on. But I want to consider just two ordinary, predictable, wondrous, vital practices: Bible reading and prayer.

And the way to think about these two practices is by the metaphor of breathing. Reading the Bible is inhaling. Praying is exhaling.

## Our Greatest Earthly Treasure

What is the Bible? It is your greatest earthly treasure. You will stand in strength, and grow in Christ, and walk in joy, and bless this world no further than you know this book.

Scripture is not an ancillary benefit for a life otherwise well-ordered, in need of a little extra boost. Scripture is shaping and fueling.

How so?

Fallen human beings enter this world *wrong*. We do not look at ourselves correctly, we do not view God correctly, we do not understand the way to be truly happy, we are ignorant of where all human history is heading, and we do not have the wisdom that makes life work well. And so on. The Christian life—our growth in Christ—is nothing other than the lifelong deconstruction of what we naturally think and assume and the reconstruction of truth through the Bible. The Bible reeducates us. The Bible makes sages out of fools. It corrects us.

But the Bible not only corrects us; it also oxygenates us. We need a Bible not only because we are wrong in our minds but also because we are empty in our souls. This is why I like the metaphor of breathing. Taking a big breath into our lungs fills us with fresh air, gives us oxygen, calms us down, provides focus, and brings mental clarity. What inhaling does for us physically, Bible reading does for us spiritually.

In this shifty, uncertain world, God has given us actual words. Concrete, unmoving, fixed words. We can go to the rock of Scripture amid the shifting sands of this life. Your Bible is going to have the same words tomorrow that it does today. Friends can't provide that—they will move in and out of your life, loyal today but absent tomorrow. Parents and their counsel will die. Your pastor will not always be available to take your call. The counselor who has given you such sage instruction will one day retire, or maybe you'll move out of state. But you can roll out of bed tomorrow morning and, whatever stressors slide uncomfortably across your mental horizon as you groan with the anxieties of the day, your friend the Bible is unfailingly steady. Through it God himself draws near to you.

## A Book of Good News

Many of us approach the Bible not as oxygenating, however, but as suffocating. We see the Bible lying there on the end table. We know we should open it. Sometimes we do. But it is usually with a sense of begrudged duty. Life is demanding enough, we think. Do I really need more demands?

That's an understandable feeling. But it is lamentably wrong. And it brings me to the central thing I want to say about the Bible as we continue to think about how real sinners get traction for real change in their lives. The Bible is good news, not a pep talk. *News.* It is reporting on something that has happened. The Bible is like the front page of the newspaper, not the advice column. To be sure, the Bible also has plenty of instruction. But the exhortations and commands of Scripture flow out of the Bible's central message, like ribs flowing out of a spine. Paul said that the Old Testament was written so that "through the encouragement of the Scriptures we might have hope" (Rom. 15:4). The Bible is help, not oppression. It is given to buoy us along in life, not drag us down. Our own dark thoughts of God are what cause us to shrink back from opening and yielding to it.

When we yawn over the Bible, that's like a severe asthmatic yawning over the free offer of a ventilator while gasping for air. Read the Bible asking not *mainly* whom to imitate and how to live but what it shows us about a God who loves to save and about sinners who need saving.

Every passage contributes to the single, overarching storyline of Scripture, which culminates in Jesus. Just as you wouldn't parachute into the middle of a novel, read a paragraph out of context, and expect to understand all that it means, you cannot expect to understand all that a passage of Scripture means without plotting it in the big arc of the Bible's narrative. And the main story of the Bible is that God sent his Son Jesus to do what Adam and Israel and we ourselves have failed to do—honor God and obey him fully. Every word in the Bible contributes to that message. Jesus himself said so (Luke 24:44; John 5:46).

## Exhaling

And praying is exhaling. Breathe in; breathe out. We take in the life-giving words of God, and we breathe them back out to God in prayer.

How does prayer fit in to this book? This is a book on growing in Christ. And my resounding theme is that the Christian life is at heart a matter not of doing more or behaving better but of going deeper. And the primary emphasis I have wanted to give is that we grow specifically by going deeper into the gospel, into the love of Christ and our experienced union with him. As we now think about prayer, here is what we are doing: we are reflecting on the way our own souls must go out to God in Christ to desire, to long for, to receive, to dwell in, to thank him for his endless love. The gospel comes to us in the Scriptures, and in prayer we receive and enjoy it.

Put differently, to put prayer together with Scripture reading is simply to acknowledge that God is a real person with whom believers have an actual, moment-by-moment relationship. The Bible is God speaking to us; prayer is our speaking to him. If we do not pray, we do not believe God is an actual person. We may say we do. But we don't really. If we do not pray, we actually think he is an impersonal force of some kind, distant and removed. We don't view him as a *Father*.

What would you say to a ten-year-old daughter who never spoke to her dad, never asked him for anything, never thanked him, never expressed love to him, despite his many expressions of love to her? You could only conclude that she believed she had a father only in theory, not in actuality. You could only conclude that her father's love was not *real* to her.

Move through your day praying. Let God be your moment-by-moment Father (Rom. 8:15; Gal. 4:6). Hear his voice in Scripture in the morning, and turn that Scripture into prayer— and then let that time with him, that back-and-forth communion, send you off into your day communing with him all day long.

### Inhale, Exhale

You wouldn't try to go through life holding your breath. So don't go through life without Bible reading and praying. Let your soul breathe. Oxygenate with the Bible; and breathe out the $CO_2$ of prayer as you speak back to God your wonder, your worry, and your waiting. Keep open the channel between your little life and heaven itself through the Bible and prayer.

As you do, you will grow. You won't feel it day to day. But you'll come to the end of your life a radiant man or woman. And you will have left in your wake the aroma of heaven. You will have blessed the world. Your life will have mattered.

9

# Supernaturalized

THE FATHER ORDAINS SALVATION, the Son accomplishes salvation, and the Spirit applies salvation. In other words, there is no Christian life without the Spirit. The Christian life is purely theoretical if there is no operation of the Spirit. Everything that we *experience* of God is the working of the Spirit. That is true at conversion, as the Spirit opens our eyes to our sin and Christ's saving offer. And it is true of our growth.

The main thing I want to say in this chapter is this: because of the Spirit, *you can grow*. Those feelings of futility, the sense of impossibility, the settled resignation that you have permanently plateaued—that is not of heaven but of hell. Satan loves your shrugged acquiescence to your sin. Jesus Christ's heart for you is flourishing growth. He understands more deeply than you do the psychology of the heart fueling the sin you can't seem to leave behind once and for all. And he is fully equipped to walk you out of that darkness. For he has given you the most precious gift of all: his own Holy Spirit.

If you are a Christian, you are now permanently indwelt by the Spirit, and if you are permanently indwelt by the Spirit, then you have been *supernaturalized*. If you choose to stay in your sins, you won't be able to stand before God one day and tell him he didn't provide you with the resources.

### Three Kinds of Men

But are there not plenty of decent human beings who are not indwelt by the Spirit, you may wonder? Certainly. That is because all people are created in the image of God, and by God's universal common grace he restrains much evil that would otherwise be executed.

But still, you might wonder, do we really need the Spirit in order to live a moral life? The answer is that we do not need the Spirit to live a moral life, but we do need the Spirit to live a supernatural life. In other words, we don't need the Spirit to be different on the outside; we do need the Spirit to be different on the inside.

So we can stiff-arm God by breaking all the rules, or we can stiff-arm God by keeping all his rules but doing so begrudgingly.

C. S. Lewis brilliantly captures this in his little essay "Three Kinds of Men." He says that there are not two but three kinds of people in the world. The first consists of those who live purely for themselves, and all that they do serves their own selfish cares. The second kind are those who acknowledge that there is some code outside them that they should follow—whether conscience or the Ten Commandments or what their parents taught them or whatever. Lewis says that people of this second kind see this other moral claim on them but feel a tension between that external moral claim and their own natural desires. As a result they are constantly swiveling back and forth between pursuing their own desires and following this higher claim. Lewis insightfully relates this tension to that of paying a tax—people in this second category pay their taxes faithfully but hope that something will be left over for them to spend on themselves.

Some people throw out all rules (group 1). Others try to keep all the rules (group 2). Neither approach is New Testament Christianity. The third kind of person is operating on a different plane entirely. Lewis puts it like this:

> The third class is of those who can say like St Paul that for them "to live is Christ." These people have got rid of the tiresome business of adjusting the rival claims of Self and God by the simple expedient of rejecting the claims of Self altogether.

The old egoistic will has been turned round, reconditioned, and made into a new thing. The will of Christ no longer limits theirs; it is theirs. All their time, in belonging to Him, belongs also to them, for they are His.[1]

Lewis goes on to conclude that it is simplistic to view only two kinds of people, the disobedient and the obedient. For we can be "obedient" in the sense that we follow a certain code, yet in a taxpaying kind of way. Authentic Christianity is not simply doing mechanically what God says but enjoying God. "The price of Christ is something, in a way, much easier than moral effort—it is to want Him."[2]

The point of this book on growing in Christ is to help Christians leave behind the second kind of person Lewis describes here and to be melted, more and more deeply, into the third kind of person. And here's the point: we only get from person 2 to person 3 through the Holy Spirit. To grow as a disciple of Christ is not adding Christ *to* your life but collapsing into Christ *as* your life. He's not a new top priority, competing with the other claims of reputation, finances, and sexual gratification. He is asking you to embrace the freefall of total abandon to his purpose in your life. And that is why the Holy Spirit dwells within you. He is the one who is empowering you to do what would be utterly impossible left to carnal resources—to step into the delicious, terrifying freedom of single-minded allegiance to Jesus.

It may feel impossible to you to do that. That's good. It *is* impossible. You'll never get there until you first try living for Christ out of your own strength and discover just how fearful and cautious and spiritually impotent you are on your own steam. It's then, as you give up on yourself and throw your hands up in the air, that your heart is most fertile for the supernaturalizing power of the Holy Spirit.

Closed vents can't be cleaned, full cups can't be filled, and the Spirit does not enter where we are quietly operating out of self-dependence. But the distraught, the empty, the pleading, the self-despairing, those tired of paying the tax of obedience to God and trying to live on what's left over—theirs are hearts irresistible to the humble Holy Spirit.

## A Foretaste of Heaven

Keep in step with the person of the Holy Spirit. Ask the Father to fill you with the Spirit. Look to Christ, in the power of the Spirit. Open yourself up to the Spirit. Consecrate yourself to the beautiful Spirit's ways in your life. Recognize and believe way down deep in your heart that without the empowering Spirit all your ministry and efforts and evangelizing and attempts to kill sin will be in vain.

As you do so, you will be a little walking portrait of heaven itself to everyone around you. With lots of foibles and mistakes, for sure. And many lapses back into walking in the flesh—like Lewis's second kind of man. But here and there, at first for short bursts but gradually for longer stretches of your day, you will be learning to operate out of God's own divine resources. You will be giving people a taste of Jesus himself, the Lord whose Spirit has taken up residence within you.

# Conclusion: What Now?

THE FINAL CONCLUSION, the deepest secret, to growing in Christ is this: look to him. Set your gaze upon him. Abide in him, hour by hour. Draw strength from his love. He is a person, not a concept. Become personally acquainted with him, ever more deeply as the years roll by.

It may seem, at this point in the book, that its nine chapters have given you a list of nine strategies to implement or nine different techniques to bear in mind. That's not at all what I want ringing in your heart as you close this short book. I do not have nine things to say. I have one thing to say. Look to Christ. You will grow in Christ as you direct your gaze to Christ. If you take your eyes off of Jesus Christ and direct your gaze to your own growth, you will prevent the very growth you desire.

On September 10, 1760, John Newton wrote to a "Miss Medhurst," who was one of a group of women Newton had visited in Yorkshire to offer spiritual counsel. Responding to her and her friends' request for help in going deeper with the Lord, he said:

> The best advice I can send, or the best wish I can form for you, is that you may have an abiding and experimental sense of those words of the apostle which are just now upon my mind—"*Looking unto Jesus*." The duty, the privilege, the safety, the unspeakable happiness, of a believer, are all comprised in that one sentence. . . . Looking unto Jesus is the object that melts the soul into love and gratitude.[1]

My goal in this book has simply been to coach you into that single, simple, all-determining impulse of the heart: looking to Jesus. If you look to him, everything else is footnotes. All else will fall into place. If you do not look to Jesus, no amount of techniques or strategies will finally help you; all will be for nothing. Peel back every layer of distraction and look to Christ. Simplify your heart and all its cares. Look to Christ and his overflowing heart.

Let your union and communion with Jesus Christ, the friend of sinners, take you deeper, ever deeper, into the wonders of the gospel. And watch your heart, and therefore your whole life, blossom.

# Acknowledgments

THANK YOU, MIKE REEVES, for inviting me to contribute this book to the Union series. This partnership, and the friendship it reflects, is precious to me.

Thank you, Davy Chu, Drew Hunter, and Wade Urig, brother pastors whom I revere, for reading and improving the manuscript. I love you.

Thank you, dearest Stacey, for insisting that I keep writing and for encouraging me all along the way. I adore you.

Thank you, Crossway, for your care of this project from start to finish.

Thank you, Thom Notaro, for your wonderful partnership in this project as its editor.

I dedicate this book to my seminary professors. When I landed on the campus of Covenant Theological Seminary in St. Louis in August 2002, I could hardly believe what I was seeing: men of God whose erudition and learning and commitment to the doctrines of grace *took them down deeper into humility and love.* I could have learned Greek anywhere; I could only learn interpersonal beauty fueled by Reformed theology at Covenant, under the faculty who were there at that time. They gave me a theological foundation for understanding how I grow as a Christian. But then, more wondrously, they gave me living pictures of what such growth blossoms into. In this Mordor of a world, I found myself in the Shire. What a mercy for God to send me there. I needed it. I still do. Thank you, dear fathers and brothers.

# Notes

*Chapter 2: Despair*

1. *Letters of John Newton* (Edinburgh: Banner of Truth, 2007), 184.

*Chapter 4: Embrace*

1. Thomas Goodwin, *The Heart of Christ* (Edinburgh: Banner of Truth, 2011), 61.

*Chapter 5: Acquittal*

1. Thomas Adam, *Private Thoughts on Religion* (Glasgow: Collins, 1824), 199.
2. James S. Stewart, *A Man in Christ: The Vital Elements of St. Paul's Religion* (New York: Harper & Row, 1935), 258–60.
3. G. C. Berkouwer, *Faith and Sanctification*, trans. John Vriend, Studies in Dogmatics (Grand Rapids, MI: Eerdmans, 1952), 93.

*Chapter 7: Pain*

1. John Owen, *Overcoming Sin and Temptation*, ed. Kelly M. Kapic and Justin Taylor (Wheaton, IL: Crossway, 2006), 50.

2. C. S. Lewis, *The Collected Letters of C. S. Lewis*, vol. 3, *Narnia, Cambridge, and Joy, 1950–1963*, ed. Walter Hooper (San Francisco: HarperCollins, 2009), 507; emphasis original.

*Chapter 9: Supernaturalized*

1. C. S. Lewis, "Three Kinds of Men," in *Present Concerns* (London: Fount, 1986), 21. For similar articulations of what Lewis is after, though none quite as penetratingly clear as his, see Martin Luther, *Career of the Reformer III*, in *Luther's Works*, ed. Jaroslav Pelikan and Helmut T. Lehmann, 55 vols. (Philadelphia: Fortress, 1955–1986), 33:318; Luther, *The Christian in Society I*, in *Luther's Works*, 44:235–42 (cf. Luther, *Lectures on Galatians 1–4*, in *Luther's Works*, 26:125); Adolf Schlatter, *The Theology of the Apostles*, trans. Andreas J. Köstenberger (Grand Rapids, MI: Baker, 1997), 102; Geerhardus Vos, "Alleged Legalism in Paul," in *Redemptive History and Biblical Interpretation: The Shorter Writings of Geerhardus Vos*, ed. Richard B. Gaffin Jr. (Phillipsburg, NJ: Presbyterian and Reformed, 1980), 390–92; F. B. Meyer, *The Directory of the Devout Life: Meditations on the Sermon on the Mount* (New York: Revell, 1904), 148–51; Herman Ridderbos, *Paul: An Outline of His Theology* (Grand Rapids: Eerdmans, 1975), 137–40; Søren Kierkegaard, as quoted in Clare Carlisle, *Kierkegaard: A Guide for the Perplexed* (London: Continuum, 2007), 77–83; Martyn Lloyd-Jones, *Experiencing the New Birth: Studies in John 3* (Wheaton, IL: Crossway, 2015), 289.

2. Lewis, "Three Kinds of Men," 22.

*Conclusion: What Now?*

1. *Letters of John Newton* (Edinburgh: Banner of Truth, 2007), 47–48.

# Scripture Index

# Union

**We fuel reformation in churches and lives.**

Union Publishing invests in the next generation of leaders with theology that gives them a taste for a deeper knowledge of God. From books to our free online content, we are committed to producing excellent resources that will refresh, transform, and grow believers and their churches.

We want people everywhere to know, love, and enjoy God, glorifying him in everything they do. For this reason, we've collected hundreds of free articles, podcasts, book chapters, and video content for our free online collection. We also produce a fresh stream of written, audio, and video resources to help you to be more fully alive in the truth, goodness, and beauty of Jesus.

If you are hungry for reformational resources that will help you delight in God and grow in Christ, we'd love for you to visit us at unionpublishing.org.

**unionpublishing.org**

# Union Series

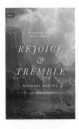  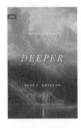 

**FULL EDITION**
*Rejoice and Tremble*

**CONCISE EDITION**
*What Does It Mean to Fear the Lord?*

**FULL EDITION**
*Deeper*

**CONCISE EDITION**
*How Does God Change Us?*

The Union series invites readers to experience deeper enjoyment of God through four interconnected values: delighting in God, growing in Christ, serving the church, and blessing the world.

For more information, visit **crossway.org**.

"Modern people often view the fear of God with disdainful suspicion, but Michael Reeves shows us that godly fear is really nothing other than love for God as God. Reeves also helps us to see that the greatest factor in promoting the fear of God is knowing his grace in Christ. As John Bunyan said, 'There is nothing in heaven or earth that can so awe the heart as the grace of God.' This wonderful book not only teaches but sings, leading us to 'rejoice with trembling' (Ps. 2:11)."

**Joel R. Beeke,** President and Professor of Systematic Theology and Homiletics, Puritan Reformed Theological Seminary

"We used to sing a hymn that said, 'O how I fear Thee, living God! With deepest, tenderest fears.' No longer. But the hymn's first lines remind us of what we are missing: 'My God, how wonderful Thou art, Thy majesty, how bright.' Only those who find God to be 'wonderful' and his majesty 'bright' experience the 'tenderest' fear. So we have a problem; but thankfully help is at hand in *What Does It Mean to Fear the Lord?* Like an elder brother, Michael Reeves guides us into a fresh understanding of the fear of the Lord. On the way, he introduces us to some of his friends—masters in the school of discipleship—who have walked the path before us. Join him on the journey. You will soon discover why 'the Lord takes pleasure in those who fear him' (Ps. 147:11)."

**Sinclair B. Ferguson,** Chancellor's Professor of Systematic Theology, Reformed Theological Seminary

"The fear of the Lord is the beginning of wisdom, the Bible says, and reading this book will make you wise—wise to who God is and what God requires of us by way of loving, responsive discipleship. Packed full of historical nuggets, *What Does It Mean to Fear the Lord?* deserves to be widely read. 'Walking in the fear of the Lord' is language that has largely disappeared from the contemporary church. The result is the insipid quality of a great deal of current Christianity. Recapturing the sense of God's incomprehensible greatness and holiness is the needed antidote this book provides. An absolute gem of a book."

**Derek W. H. Thomas,** Senior Minister, First Presbyterian Church, Columbia, South Carolina; Chancellor's Professor of Systematic and Pastoral Theology, Reformed Theological Seminary

"Ours is a day of great fears—fear of financial collapse, fear of terrorist attacks, fear of climatic disasters, fear of a deadly pandemic—all kinds of fears, except the most important of all: the reverential fear of God. How needed then is this marvelous study of a much-neglected theme, one that is central to the Scriptures and vital to human flourishing."

**Michael A. G. Haykin,** Chair and Professor of Church History, The Southern Baptist Theological Seminary

"Michael Reeves has given us something we badly need and likely haven't realized—a fresh encounter with the thrilling fear of the Lord. This book will bring renewed devotion and delight. Having read it, I can't wait to read it again!"

**Sam Allberry,** apologist; Associate Pastor, Immanuel Church, Nashville, Tennessee

*WHAT DOES IT MEAN*
*TO FEAR THE LORD?*

**Union**

A book series edited by Michael Reeves

# WHAT DOES IT MEAN TO FEAR THE LORD?

*MICHAEL REEVES*

**CROSSWAY®**

WHEATON, ILLINOIS

**Library of Congress Cataloging-in-Publication Data**
Names: Reeves, Michael (Michael Richard Ewert), author.
Title: What does it mean to fear the Lord? / Michael Reeves.
Description: Wheaton, Illinois : Crossway, 2021. | Series: Union | Includes bibliographical references and index.
Identifiers: LCCN 2020027787 (print) | LCCN 2020027788 (ebook) | ISBN 9781433565366 (trade paperback) | ISBN 9781433565373 (pdf) | ISBN 9781433565380 (mobipocket) | ISBN 9781433565397 (epub)
Subjects: LCSH: God (Christianity)—Worship and love. | Fear of God—Christianity.
Classification: LCC BV4817 .R44 2021 (print) | LCC BV4817 (ebook) | DDC 231.7—dc23
LC record available at https://lccn.loc.gov/2020027787
LC ebook record available at https://lccn.loc.gov/2020027788

Crossway is a publishing ministry of Good News Publishers.

| VP | | 30 | 29 | 28 | 27 | 26 | 25 | 24 | 23 | 22 | 21 |
|----|----|----|----|----|----|----|----|----|----|----|----|
| 15 | 14 | 13 | 12 | 11 | 10 | 9 | 8 | 7 | 6 | 5 | 4 | 3 | 2 |

*For Rob and John, my dear friends*

———

In a perfect Friendship this Appreciative Love is, I think, often so great and so firmly based that each member of the circle feels, in his secret heart, humbled before all the rest. Sometimes he wonders what he is doing there among his betters. He is lucky beyond desert to be in such company. Especially when the whole group is together, each bringing out all that is best, wisest, or funniest in all the others. Those are the golden sessions; when four or five of us after a hard day's walking have come to our inn; when our slippers are on, our feet spread out towards the blaze and our drinks at our elbows; when the whole world, and something beyond the world, opens itself to our minds as we talk; and no one has any claim on or any responsibility for another, but all are free-men and equals as if we had first met an hour ago, while at the same time an Affection mellowed by the years enfolds us. Life—natural life—has no better gift to give. Who could have deserved it?

<small>C. S. LEWIS</small>, *The Four Loves*

# Contents

# Series Preface

OUR INNER CONVICTIONS AND VALUES shape our lives and
our ministries. And at Union—the cooperative ministries of
Union School of Theology, Union Publishing, Union Research, and Union Mission (visit www.theolo.gy)—we long
to grow and support men and women who will delight in
God, grow in Christ, serve the church, and bless the world.
This Union series of books is an attempt to express and share
those values.

They are values that flow from the beauty and grace of God.
The living God is so glorious and kind, he cannot be known
without being adored. Those who truly know him will love
him, and without that heartfelt delight in God, we are nothing but hollow hypocrites. That adoration of God necessarily
works itself out in a desire to grow in Christlikeness. It also
fuels a love for Christ's precious bride, the church, and a desire

humbly to serve—rather than use—her. And, lastly, loving God brings us to share his concerns, especially to see his life-giving glory fill the earth.

Each exploration of a subject in the Union series will appear in two versions: a full volume and a concise one. The concise treatments, such as this one, are like shorter guided tours: they stick to the main streets and move on fast. You may find, at the end of this little book, that you have questions or want to explore some more: in that case, the fuller volume will take you further up and further in.

My hope and prayer is that these books will bless you and your church as you develop a deeper delight in God that overflows in joyful integrity, humility, Christlikeness, love for the church, and a passion to make disciples of all nations.

*Michael Reeves*
SERIES EDITOR

# 1

# Do Not Be Afraid!

BOO!

It's one of the first words we enjoy. As children, we loved to leap out on our friends and shout it. But at the same time, we were scared of the dark and the monsters under the bed. We were both fascinated *and* repelled by our fears. And not much changes when we grow up: adults love scary movies and thrills that bring us face-to-face with our worst fears. But we also agonize over all the dreadful things that could happen to us: how we could lose our lives, health, or loved ones; how we might fail or be rejected. Fear is probably the strongest human emotion. But it baffles us.

## To Fear or Not to Fear?

When we come to the Bible, the picture seems equally confusing: is fear a good thing or bad? Many times Scripture clearly views fear as a bad thing from which Christ has come to rescue us. The apostle John writes: "There is no fear in love, but perfect love casts out fear. For fear has to do with punishment, and whoever fears has not been perfected in love" (1 John 4:18). Indeed, the most frequent command in Scripture is "Do not be afraid!"

Yet, again and again in Scripture we are called to fear. Even more strangely, we are called to fear *God*. The verse that quickly comes to mind is Proverbs 9:10, "The fear of the LORD is the beginning of wisdom." In the New Testament, Jesus describes the unrighteous judge as one "who neither feared God nor respected man" (Luke 18:2). Paul writes, "Let us cleanse ourselves from every defilement of body and spirit, bringing holiness to completion in the fear of God" (2 Cor. 7:1).

All of which can leave us rather confused. On the one hand, we are told that Christ frees us from fear; on the other, we are told we ought to fear—and fear God, no less. It can leave us wishing that "the fear of God" were not so prominent an idea in Scripture. We have enough fears without adding more, thank you very much. And fearing God just feels so negative, it doesn't seem to square with the God of love we meet in the gospel. Why would any God worth loving *want* to be feared?

My aim now is to cut through this confusion. I want you to rejoice in this paradox that the gospel both frees us from fear and gives us fear. It frees us from our crippling fears, giving us instead a most delightful fear. And I want to show that for Christians "the fear of God" really does *not* mean being afraid of God.

Indeed, Scripture will have many hefty surprises in store for us as it describes the fear of God. Take just one example for now. In Isaiah 11:1–3 we are given a beautiful description of the Messiah, filled with the Spirit:

There shall come forth a shoot from the stump of Jesse,
    and a branch from his roots shall bear fruit.
And the Spirit of the LORD shall rest upon him,
    the Spirit of wisdom and understanding,
    the Spirit of counsel and might,
    the Spirit of knowledge and the fear of the LORD.
And his delight shall be in the fear of the LORD.

Those last two statements should make us question what this fear of the Lord is. Here we see that the fear of the Lord is not something the Messiah wishes to be without. Even he has the fear of the Lord—but he is not reluctant about it. Quite the opposite: his *delight* is in the fear of the Lord. It forces us to ask, what is this fear, that it can be Christ's very delight? It cannot be a negative, gloomy duty.

15

## Today's Culture of Fear

But before we dive into the good news the Bible has about our fears and the fear of God, it is worth noticing how anxious our culture has become. Seeing where our society now is can help us understand why we have a problem with fear—and why the fear of God is just the tonic we need.

These days, it seems, everyone is talking about a culture of fear. From Twitter to television, we fret about global terrorism, extreme weather, and political turmoil. Our private lives are filled with still more sources of anxiety. Take our diet, for example. If you choose the full-fat version on the menu, you're heading for a heart attack. Yet we keep discovering that the low-calorie alternative is actually carcinogenic or harmful in some other way. And so a low-grade fear starts with breakfast. Or think of the paranoia surrounding parenting today. The valid but usually overblown fear of the kidnapper lurking online or outside every school has helped fuel the rise of helicopter parenting and children more and more fenced in to keep them safe. As a whole, we are an increasingly anxious and uncertain culture.

And therein is an extraordinary paradox, for we live more safely than ever before. Though we are safer than almost any other society in history, safety has become the holy grail of our culture. And like *the* Holy Grail, it is something we can never quite reach. Protected like never before, we are skittish and panicky like never before.

How can this be? Quite simply, our culture has lost God as the proper object of fear. That fear of God (as I hope to show) was a happy and healthy fear that controlled our other fears, reining in anxiety. With our society having lost God as the proper object of healthy fear, our culture is necessarily becoming more neurotic and anxious. In ousting God from our culture, other concerns—from personal health to the health of the planet—have assumed a divine ultimacy in our minds. Good things have become cruel and pitiless idols. And thus we feel helplessly fragile, and society fills with anxieties.

## The Fearful Legacy of Atheism

The suggestion that loss of the fear of God is the root cause of our culture's anxiety is a real blow to atheism. For atheism sold the idea that if you liberate people from belief in God, that will liberate them from fear. But throwing off the fear of God has not made our society happier and less fretful. Quite the opposite.

So, what does our culture do with all its anxiety? Given its essentially secular self-identity, our culture will not turn to God. The only possible solution, then, must be for us to sort it out ourselves. Thus, Western society has medicalized fear. Fear has become an elusive disease to be medicated. (I do not mean to imply here that use of drugs to curb anxiety is wrong—only that they are a palliative, at times an important one, and not an ultimate solution.)[1] Yet that attempt to eradicate fear as we would eradicate a disease has effectively made comfort (complete absence of fear) a health category—or even a moral category. Where discomfort was once considered quite normal (and quite proper for certain situations), it is now deemed an essentially unhealthy thing.

It means that in a culture awash with anxiety, fear is increasingly seen as *wholly* negative. And Christians have been swept along, adopting society's negative assessment of all fear. Small wonder, then, that we shy away from talking about the fear of God, despite its prominence in Scripture. It is understandable, but it is tragic: the loss of the fear of God is what ushered in our age of anxiety, but the fear of God is the very antidote to our fretfulness.

## A Rose by Any Other Name Would Smell as Sweet

The fact is that not all fear is the same, or unhealthy, or unpleasant. We must distinguish between different sorts of fear, between wrong fear and right fear. That is what we will do now. Then we can rejoice in the fact that the fear of God is not like fears that torment us. Then we can appreciate how it is the one positive, wonderful fear that deals with our anxieties.

2

# Sinful Fear

WE ALL KNOW FEAR. When you experience fear, your body reacts: you feel the adrenaline release as your heart races, your breathing accelerates, and your muscles tense. Sometimes that can be intensely fun: think of the rush of the roller coaster or the big game. Sometimes it can be terrifying as panic grips you so utterly, you cannot think but only shake, sweat, and fret. Underneath those experiences are common thoughts. Our different fears have common traits, a common DNA.

However, it is important to recognize that there are different *sorts* of fear. Confusion on this point is deadly. Take, for example, how some Christians see the lack of reverence and awe of God in our churches and seem to think the answer is to make people *afraid* of God. As if our love for God needs to be tempered by being *afraid* of him.

Scripture speaks quite differently. Take, for example, Exodus 20, where the people of Israel gather at Mount Sinai:

> Now when all the people saw the thunder and the flashes of lightning and the sound of the trumpet and the mountain smoking, the people were afraid and trembled, and they stood far off and said to Moses, "You speak to us, and we will listen; but do not let God speak to us, lest we die." Moses said to the people, "*Do not fear*, for God has come to test you, *that the fear of him may be before you*, that you may not sin." (vv. 18–20)

Moses here sets out a contrast between being *afraid* of God and *fearing* God: those who have the fear of him will not be afraid of him. Yet he uses the same "fear" word for both. Evidently there is a fear of God that is desirable, and there is a fear of God that is not.

Let's have a look now at the different types of fear of God we meet in Scripture.

## Sinful Fear

The first type of fear of God is condemned by Scripture. I have been tempted to call it "wrong fear," but there is a sense in which it is quite right for unbelievers to be afraid of God. The holy God *is* terrible to those who are far from him. Instead, I am calling it "sinful fear," since it is a fear of God that flows from sin.

This sinful fear of God is the sort of fear James tells us the demons have when they believe and shudder (James 2:19). It is the fear Adam had when he first sinned and hid from God (Gen. 3:10). Sinful fear drives you *away* from God. This is the fear of the unbeliever who hates God, who fears being exposed as a sinner and so runs from God.

This is the fear of God that it is at odds with love for God. It is the fear rooted in the very heart of sin. Dreading and retreating from God, this fear generates the doubt that rationalizes unbelief. It is the motor for both atheism and idolatry, inspiring people to invent alternative "realities" in place of the living God. Take, for example, the late Christopher Hitchens, one of the "four horsemen" of the early twenty-first-century "New Atheism." Hitchens preferred to describe himself as an "anti-theist" because he was opposed to the very possibility of God's existence. But this anti-theism, he was clear, was motivated by a fear of God. Asked on Fox News what he thought about the possibility of God's existence, he replied:

> I think it would be rather awful if it was true. If there was a permanent, total, round-the-clock divine supervision and invigilation of everything you did, you would never have a waking or sleeping moment when you weren't being watched and controlled and supervised by some celestial entity from

the moment of your conception to the moment of your death. . . . It would be like living in North Korea.[1]

Hitchens tragically misunderstood God and so feared God.

## Misunderstanding God

The experience of Christopher Hitchens shows that this sinful fear that flees from God arises in good part from a misunderstanding of him. The unfaithful servant in Jesus's parable of the ten minas displays exactly this problem when he unfairly complains to his master, "I was afraid of you, because you are a severe man" (Luke 19:21). He sees nothing of his master's kindness: in his shortsighted eyes the great man is all stingy severity, and so the servant is simply afraid.

This is the blindness Satan loves to inflict on our understanding of God. Satan would present God as pure threat. For then, when we perceive God that way, we will run from him in fear.

Yet while this fear drives people away from their Maker, it does not always drive them away from religion. Having presented God as harsh and dreadful, this fear gives people the mindset of a reluctant slave who obeys his master not out of any love but purely from fear of the whip. Out of slavish fear, people will perform all manner of duties to appease a God they secretly despise. To all the world they can seem devout, exemplary Christians, if rather lacking in joy.

## The Dread of Holiness

Another part of this sinful fear is the fear of letting go of sin, or what we might call the dread of holiness. C. S. Lewis explored this idea in *The Great Divorce*, a story that starts in the grey town (hell). While everyone there is afraid of the dark, few dare step aboard the bus to heaven, because they are even more afraid of the light. While the darkness shrouds nameless horrors, the light is more scary because it exposes them.

When the bus arrives in the bright beauty of the heavenly meadow, one of the spectral souls from hell screams, "I don't like it. . . . It gives me the pip!"[2] Then the Solid People—the residents of heaven—arrive, at which, Lewis writes, "two of the ghosts screamed and ran for the bus."[3] Their very splendor is terrifying to the shrunken wraiths from hell.

> "Go away!" squealed the Ghost. "Go away! Can't you see I want to be alone?"
>
> "But you need help," said the Solid One.
>
> "If you have the least trace of decent feeling left," said the Ghost, "you'll keep away. I don't want help. I want to be left alone."[4]

The fear, for the ghosts, is their realization that to dwell in heaven they must give up their "dignity" or self-dependence, their misery, their anger, their grumbles. They cannot imagine being without the very things that deform them and keep them from happiness, and they shudder at the prospect of liberation and purification. Their fear is a struggle against joy. It is a fear of the light and a refusal to let go of the darkness.

It is the very richness and energy of the pure life of heaven that is so overwhelming and fearful to the ghosts. They will do almost anything to avoid it. Sinners prefer their darkness and chains to the light and freedom of heaven, and so they dread its holiness.

### Sinful Fear in Christians

Sadly, Christians are not immune to this sinful fear. Poor teaching, hard times, and Satan's accusations can all feed this cringing fear of God. What weed killer can we use? Really, the rest of this book is an attempt to hold out the deeper cure.

It is the devil's work to promote a fear of God that makes people afraid of God such that they want to flee from God. The Spirit's work is the exact opposite: to produce in us a wonderful fear that wins and draws us *to* God. It is to this happy, Scripture-commended, Spirit-breathed fear that we turn now.

3

# Right Fear

C. I. SCOFIELD ONCE CALLED *the fear of God* "a phrase of Old Testament piety."[1] And so it was. However, *the fear of God* is not a phrase of Old Testament piety *only*, for the right fear of God is, quite explicitly, a blessing of the new covenant. Speaking of the new covenant, the Lord promised through Jeremiah:

> And they shall be my people, and I will be their God. I will give them one heart and one way, that they may fear me forever, for their own good and the good of their children after them. I will make with them an everlasting covenant, that I will not turn away from doing good to them. *And I will put the fear of me in their hearts, that they may not turn from me.* (Jer. 32:38–40)

What is this fear that the Lord will put in the hearts of his people? Unlike that devilish fear we have seen that would drive us away from God, this is a fear that keeps us from turning away from him.

## An Unexpected Fear

In Jeremiah 33, the Lord goes on to explain this fear in words so striking they overturn all our expectations. He promises:

> I will cleanse them from all the guilt of their sin against me, and I will forgive all the guilt of their sin and rebellion against me. And this city shall be to me a name of joy, a praise and a glory before all the nations of the earth who shall hear of all the good that I do for them. They shall fear and tremble *because of all the good and all the prosperity I provide for it*. (vv. 8–9)

This is not a fear of punishment. Quite the opposite: in Jeremiah 33, the Lord promises to cleanse his people, forgive them, and do great good for them. And they fear and tremble precisely *because of* all the good he does for them.

Here is not a fear that stands on the flip side of the grace and goodness of God. It is the sort of fear Hosea describes when he prophesies how "the children of Israel shall return and seek the LORD their God, and David their king, *and they shall come in fear to the LORD and to his goodness in the latter days*" (Hos.

3:5). It is a fear that, as Charles Spurgeon put it, "leans toward the Lord" *because of* his very goodness.[2]

Take another surprising example of this fear, from when the Lord appears to Jacob at Bethel. Again, the Lord utters not one word of threat but only promise after promise of grace:

> Jacob left Beersheba and went toward Haran. And he came to a certain place and stayed there that night, because the sun had set. Taking one of the stones of the place, he put it under his head and lay down in that place to sleep. And he dreamed, and behold, there was a ladder set up on the earth, and the top of it reached to heaven. And behold, the angels of God were ascending and descending on it! And behold, the LORD stood above it and said, "I am the LORD, the God of Abraham your father and the God of Isaac. The land on which you lie I will give to you and to your offspring. Your offspring shall be like the dust of the earth, and you shall spread abroad to the west and to the east and to the north and to the south, and in you and your offspring shall all the families of the earth be blessed. Behold, I am with you and will keep you wherever you go, and will bring you back to this land. For I will not leave you until I have done what I have promised you." Then Jacob awoke from his sleep and said, "Surely the LORD is in this place, and I did not know

it." And he was afraid and said, "How awesome [fearful] is this place! This is none other than the house of God, and this is the gate of heaven." (Gen. 28:10–17)

The Lord promises to bless and increase Jacob, to be with him and to keep him, never to leave him, and to fulfill all his good purposes for him. And in the face of pure goodness and absolute grace, Jacob *fears*. John Bunyan concluded that this right fear flows primarily

> from a sense of the love and kindness of God to the soul . . . from some sense or hope of mercy from God by Jesus Christ. . . . Indeed nothing can lay a stronger obligation upon the heart to fear God, than sense of, or hope in mercy (Jer 33:8, 9). This begetteth true tenderness of heart, true godly softness of spirit; this truly endeareth the affections to God; and in this true tenderness, softness, and endearedness of affection to God, lieth the very essence of this fear of the Lord.[3]

## Fear and Love

Clearly, the fear of God is not at all what we, with our culture's allergic reaction to the concept of fear, might expect. Instead, it is, as Spurgeon said, the "sort of fear which has in it the very essence of love, and without which there would be no joy even in the presence of God."[4] In fact, the closer we look, the closer fear of God and love of God appear. Sometimes fear of God and love of God are put in parallel, as in Psalm 145:

> He fulfills the desire of *those who fear him*;
>> he also hears their cry and saves them.
> The LORD preserves *all who love him*,
>> but all the wicked he will destroy. (vv. 19–20)

The reason it is not obvious to us that fear and love are so alike is that we easily misunderstand love. *Love* is a word bandied around in our lives. I "love" sitting in a cozy armchair reading a good book; I "love" a good laugh with my friends. And so I can blithely assume that "love" for God is just more of the same, meaning nothing more than a (perhaps vague) preference. Where some enjoy pudding, I enjoy God.

However, my love for one thing differs from my love for another because love changes according to its object. Let me illustrate with three true statements:

1. I love and have real affection for my dog.
2. I love and have real affection for my wife.
3. I love and have real affection for my God.

Each is true, but reading them together like that should make you wince. For you know there must be something terribly wrong if I mean exactly the same thing in each. You sincerely hope there is a difference. And there is: the three *loves* differ because the *objects* of the loves differ.

The living God is infinitely perfect and overwhelmingly beautiful in every way. And so we do not love him aright if our love is not a trembling, overwhelmed, and fearful love. In a sense, then, the trembling "fear of God" is a way of speaking about the intensity of our love for God.

The right fear of God, then, is not the flip side to our love for God. Nor is it one side of our reaction to God. It is not that we love God for his graciousness and fear him for his majesty. That would be a lopsided fear of God. We also love him in his holiness and tremble at the marvelousness of his mercy. True fear of God is true love for God defined.

The biblical theme of the fear of God helps us to see the *sort* of love toward God that is fitting. It shows us that God does not want passionless performance or a vague preference for him. To encounter the living God truly means that we cannot contain ourselves. He is not a truth to be known unaffectedly, or a good to be received listlessly. Seen clearly, the dazzling beauty and splendor of God must cause our hearts to quake.

## Is *Fear* the Best Word?

So is *fear* the most helpful word for this right response to God? This fear of God is a most positive thing, but it is hard for us to see that, given how negative the word *fear* seems. No wonder Christians prefer words like *awe*, *respect*, and *reverence* in place of *fear*. So, would another word capture it better?

Let's start with one of the words used for fear of God in Scripture. In the Old Testament, the same word can be used for both right and sinful fears: anything from bone-melting dread to ecstatic jubilation. It is used negatively:

> The sinners in Zion are *afraid*;
>> trembling has seized the godless. (Isa. 33:14)

And it is used positively: "*They shall fear* and tremble because of all the good and all the prosperity I provide for it" (Jer. 33:9). So, what is the common feature that enables the same word to be used for both experiences? In both verses, the word suggests a physical experience: of weak-kneed trembling, of being staggered. Now, I can tremble in quite different ways. I can shake in terror, as a soldier might under heavy fire. But I can also quake in overwhelmed adoration, as when the bridegroom first sees his bride.

If, then, we are to be faithful to Scripture's presentation of the fear of God, we should use words that encompass that spectrum of positive and negative experience. That helps us see the common feature of those fears: trembling. It shows us that the fear of God is no mild-mannered, reserved, or limp thing. It is a startlingly physical, overpowering reaction. And so, *respect* and *reverence* are simply too weak and grey to stand in as fit synonyms. *Awe* seems a much better fit, though even it doesn't quite capture the physical intensity or the exquisite delight that leans toward the Lord. In fact, these other words can be actively misleading. For example, if we simply use the word *awe*, we will tend to think of fear as a response to only God's transcendence and power, not his graciousness. Or take the word *respect*: it is a strange term for a response to God's love—and so it is an unbalanced substitute for the word *fear*. Similarly, *reverence* can sound too stiff and unresponsive. Not that these are wrong words—it is simply that they are not perfect synonyms for the fear of God.

Perhaps it is best to recognize the shortcomings of all words. The word *fear* has its own baggage, to be sure, but it is well established, and no one word can adequately and completely replace it. If people are to appreciate how the fear of God is distinct from all other fears, synonyms alone will not do: it must be unfolded and taught.

## Fear and Joy

Speaking of the happy thrill and exquisite delight of this fear is surprising language. Yet Scripture is clear that just as the fear of God defines true love for God, so it defines true joy in God.

The fear of the Lord is a *pleasure* to believers, for it is about enjoying his fearfully lovely glory.

"Blessed" or "happy"—like God—"is the one who fears the LORD always" (Prov. 28:14). Thus Nehemiah prays, "O Lord, let your ear be attentive to the prayer of your servant, and to the prayer of your servants who *delight to fear your name*" (Neh. 1:11).

This right fear of God is not the gloomy flip side to joy in God. Rather, it is a way of speaking about the sheer intensity of the saints' happiness in God. It helps us to see the *sort* of joy that is most fitting for believers. Our delight in God is not intended to be lukewarm. Our joy in God is, *at its purest*, a trembling and wonder-filled—yes, fearful—joy. For the object of our joy is so fearfully wonderful. We are made to rejoice and tremble before God, to love and enjoy him with an intensity that is fitting for him.

This pairing of joy and fear can be seen when two wise statements are put together. One speaks of "the whole duty of man," the other of "man's chief end," but both are about the purpose for which we were made. The first is from the book of Ecclesiastes where the Preacher concludes: "The end of the matter; all has been heard. Fear God and keep his commandments, for this is the whole duty of man" (Eccles. 12:13). The second statement is the first answer from the Westminster

Shorter Catechism, which tells us, "Man's chief end is to glorify God, and to enjoy him forever." They are describing the same truth. When the Preacher calls us to fear God, he is calling us precisely to the enjoyment of God that Westminster calls the chief end of man.

The nature of the living God means that the fear which pleases him is not a groveling, shrinking fear. He is no tyrant. It is an ecstasy of love and joy that senses how overwhelmingly kind and magnificent, good and true God is, and that therefore leans on him in staggered praise and faith.

4

# Overwhelmed by the Creator

THERE ARE DIFFERENT SORTS of fear, then: there is a right fear of God, and there is a sinful fear of God. But there are also different *sorts* of *right* fear of God. There is the fear of God the Creator, and then there is the fear of God the Redeemer in Christ.

## "O LORD, How Majestic Is Your Name in All the Earth!"

The first sort of right fear is the trembling response to God as Creator. It appreciates that God is splendid in his transcendence. God is holy, majestic, perfect, all-powerful, and dazzling in all his perfections. This fear considers the Creator and is left staggered, like David, asking, "What is man that you are mindful of him?" (Ps. 8:4). In the light of God's eternal magnificence, self-existence, and unswerving constancy, this fear feels what fleeting and fickle little things we are.

That trembling fear is the right reaction to the Creator. For the holiness of the Creator is not a quiet, anemic thing to be received with stained-glass voices and simpers. The holiness of the sovereign Lord is tremendous, vivid, and dazzling. *Not* to fear him would be blind foolishness. In the splendor of the Creator's majesty, we *should* be abased. In the brightness of his purity, we *should* be ashamed.

## Fear of the Creator in Unbelievers

There is a sense in which all people can know *something* of this fear of the Creator. The pantheist poet William Blake (1757–1827) poignantly expressed his fear of God in the words of "The Tyger":

> Tyger Tyger, burning bright,
> In the forests of the night;
> What immortal hand or eye,
> Could frame thy fearful symmetry? . . .
>
> And what shoulder, & what art,
> Could twist the sinews of thy heart?
> And when thy heart began to beat,
> What dread hand? & what dread feet? . . .
>
> When the stars threw down their spears
> And water'd heaven with their tears:

36

Did he smile his work to see?
Did he who made the Lamb make thee?[1]

The fearfulness of the tiger leads Blake to consider how dreadful its Creator must be. There is something right there. But Blake can see no further: he is left dreading *but not loving* the Creator.

## Fear of the Creator in Believers

Now compare Blake's words with those of the hymn-writer Isaac Watts:

Eternal power, whose high abode
Becomes the grandeur of a God,
Infinite lengths beyond the bounds
Where stars resolve their little rounds.

The lowest step around Thy seat,
Rises too high for Gabriel's feet;
In vain the tall archangel tries
To reach Thine height with wondering eyes.

Thy dazzling beauties whilst he sings,
He hides his face behind his wings,
And ranks of shining thrones around
Fall worshiping, and spread the ground.

Lord, what shall earth and ashes do?
We would adore our maker, too;
From sin and dust to Thee we cry,
The Great, the Holy, and the High!

Earth from afar has heard Thy fame,
And worms have learned to lisp Thy name;
But, O! the glories of Thy mind
Leave all our soaring thoughts behind.

God is in Heaven, and men below;
Be short our tunes, our words be few;
A sacred reverence checks our songs,
And praise sits silent on our tongues.[2]

As with Blake, there is wondering here. But all the tone is different: Watts is full of adoration. His fear is a worshipful and loving fear.

What makes for the difference? Very simply, Watts had been taken further in his knowledge of God. Not only did he have the knowledge of God the Creator; he also had the knowledge of God the Redeemer in Christ. And that knowledge of God as a humble, gracious, and compassionate *Redeemer* beautifies the sight of his transcendent majesty as *Creator*. Our wonder at the Creator's magnificence increases when we know it as the magnificence of the kindest Savior.

Charles Spurgeon argued that while believers have an adoring fear of God, "we, who believe in Jesus, are not afraid of God even as our King."[3] For we know the beautiful *character* of the one who rules: the sovereign Creator is a gracious and merciful Redeemer. Those who are taught only—or even predominantly—that God is King and Creator will be left with William Blake's dread. Only those who also get to hear of God's redeeming graciousness will begin to share Spurgeon's pleasure in his Creator.

> Gazing upon the vast expanse of waters,—looking up to the innumerable stars, examining the wing of an insect, and seeing there the matchless skill of God displayed in the minute; or standing in a thunderstorm, watching, as best you can, the flashes of lightning, and listening to the thunder of Jehovah's voice, have you not often shrunk into yourself, and said, "Great God, how terrible art thou!"—not afraid, but full of delight, like a child who rejoices to see his father's wealth, his father's wisdom, his father's power,—happy, and at home, but feeling oh, so little![4]

Spurgeon was quakingly delighted (and not afraid) because the immensity of the heavens and the complexity of the insects came from "his *father's* wealth, his *father's* wisdom, his *father's* power." He knew the Creator was his Father in Christ.

5

# Overwhelmed by the Father

## Filial Fear

"The fear of the LORD is the beginning of knowledge" (Prov. 1:7). It leads us from knowing God as the Creator to knowing him as our Redeemer and Father. By opening our eyes to know God aright, the Spirit turns our hearts to fear him with a loving, *filial* fear. That is the fear that is appropriate for Christians, who are brought by the Son to be beloved, adopted children before their heavenly Father.

Martin Luther knew well how the fatherhood of God changes how we fear God. From his earliest days, Luther had feared God with a loveless dread. As a monk, his mind was filled with the knowledge that God is righteous and hates sin; but Luther failed to see any further into who God is. Not knowing God as a kind and compassionate Father, Luther found he could not love him.

41

That changed when he began to see that God is a fatherly God. Looking back later in life Luther reflected that, as a monk, he had not actually been worshiping the right God, for it is "not enough," he then said, to know God as the Creator and Judge. Only when God is known as a loving Father is he known aright.

Through sending his Son to bring us back to himself, God has revealed himself to be loving and supremely fatherly. Luther found that not only does that give great assurance and joy—it also wins our hearts to him, for "we may look into His fatherly heart and sense how boundlessly He loves us. That would warm our hearts, setting them aglow with thankfulness."[1] In the salvation of this God we see a God we can wholeheartedly love. Through his redemption our fear is transformed from trembling, slavish terror to trembling, filial wonder.

### Jesus's Own Fear

It is Jesus's own filial fear that we are brought to share. Luke's Gospel tells us that as the boy Jesus grew, he "increased in wisdom and in stature" (2:52). Yet the *fear of the Lord is the beginning of wisdom* (Prov. 9:10). Jesus could not have grown in wisdom without the fear of the Lord.

God's great purpose in salvation was that the Son might be "the firstborn among many brothers" (Rom. 8:29), that the Son might share his sonship, bringing us with him before the one we can now enjoy as our Father. This means that not only do believers share the Son's own standing before the Father; we also share the Son's own filial delight in the fear of the Lord.

This filial fear is part of the Son's pleasurable adoration of his Father; indeed, it is the very emotional extremity of that wonder. It is not the dread of sinners before a holy Judge. It is not the awe of creatures before their tremendous Creator. It is the overwhelmed devotion of children marveling at the kindness and glory and complete magnificence of their Father.

That is why it is not *at all* the same thing as being afraid of God. The filial fear the Son shares with us is quite different from the sinner's dread of God. It is an adoration of God.

## Why It Matters

Those who do not know God as a merciful Redeemer and compassionate Father can never have the delight of a truly filial fear. At best, they can only tremble at his transcendent awesomeness as Creator. At worst, they can only shudder at the thought that there is a righteous Judge in heaven and hate him in their hearts.

In contrast, those who know that God's holiness is not just his separateness from us sinners in his righteousness or just his separateness from us creatures as Creator but also his absolute incomparability in grace, mercy, and kindness—they see the completeness of the beauty of holiness. They see the most glory.

They see the glory of the cross, the glory of a loving Savior, the glory of a mighty but humble God who is not ashamed to call himself their Father.

It all means that we must keep a careful eye on how we think of God. For the very shape of the gospel we proclaim will tell of how we think of God. Think of the gospel presentation that only describes God as Creator and ruler: sin is no deeper a matter than breaking his rules; redemption is about being brought back under his rulership. Such a gospel could never impart a *filial* fear and wonder, for there is no mention of God's fatherhood or our adoption in his Son. Such a gospel can only leave people with a fear of the Creator.

Only when we are resolutely Christ-centered can we tell a richer, truer gospel. Only then does the story make sense that our sin is a deeper matter than external disobedience, that it is a relational matter of our hearts loving what is wrong. Only then will we speak of God the Father sending forth his Son that he might bring us as children into his family. Only that Christ-centered gospel can draw people to share Jesus's own fear.

When Christians misunderstand the right fear of God as nothing but the fear of the Creator, they rob themselves of their filial fear. It is all too easy to see God's grandeur as Creator—which is absolutely right to do—but then fail to look to the gospel and God's grandeur as a compassionate Savior. In such thinking, God may appear great, but he will not appear good.

Those who know God as Father can have a deeper enjoyment and fear of God. See, for example, how Charles Spurgeon's filial fear of his heavenly Father enriched his wonder at the awesomeness of God as Creator. Spurgeon declared, "I love the lightnings, God's thunder is my delight."

> Men are by nature afraid of the heavens; the superstitious dread the signs in the sky, and even the bravest spirit is sometimes made to tremble when the firmament is ablaze with lightning, and the pealing thunder seems to make the vast concave of heaven to tremble and to reverberate; but I always feel ashamed to keep indoors when the thunder shakes the solid earth, and the lightnings flash like arrows from the sky. Then God is abroad, and I love to walk out in some wide space, and to look up and mark the opening gates of heaven, as the lightning reveals far beyond, and enables me to gaze into the unseen. *I like to hear my Heavenly Father's voice in the thunder.*[2]

Spurgeon could relish the transcendence and creative power of God with a trembling pleasure precisely because he saw them as the transcendence and power not just of a righteous Creator but also of his loving Father. The wonders of creation are best enjoyed by the self-conscious children of God. Lightnings, mountains, stars, and wild oceans are all more marvelous to those who see them all as the works of their majestic and gracious Father.

6

# How to Grow in This Fear

THE FEAR OF GOD is not a state of mind you can guarantee with five easy steps. It is not something that can be acquired with simple self-effort. The fear of God is a matter of the heart.

## A Matter of the Heart

How easily we can mistake the reality of the fear of God for an outward and hollow show! As Martin Luther put it: "To fear God is not merely to fall upon your knees. Even a godless man and a robber can do that."[1] Scripture presents the fear of God as a matter of the heart's inclinations. So, reads Psalm 112:1,

Blessed is the man who fears the LORD,
who greatly *delights* in his commandments!

The one who fears the Lord, then, is not merely one who grudgingly attempts the outward action of keeping the Lord's commandments. The one who truly fears the Lord greatly delights in God's commandments!

In other words, fear runs deeper than behavior: it *drives* behavior. Sinful fear *hates* God and *therefore* acts sinfully. Right fear *loves* God and therefore has a sincere longing to be like him.

The fear of God as a biblical theme stops us from thinking that we are made for either passionless performance or a detached knowledge of abstract truths. It shows that we are made to know God in such a way that our hearts tremble at his beauty and splendor. It shows us that entering the life of Christ involves a transformation of our very affections, so that we begin actually to despise—and not merely renounce—the sins we once cherished, and treasure the God we once abhorred.

This is why singing is such an appropriate expression of a right, filial fear. "Clap your hands, all peoples!" cry the sons of Korah in Psalm 47;

> Shout to God with loud songs of joy!
> *For the* Lord, *the Most High, is to be feared.* (vv. 1–2;
> see also Ps. 96:1–4)

In fact, the fear of the Lord is the reason Christianity is the most song-filled of all religions. It is the reason why, from how

Christians worship together to how they stream music, they are always looking to make melody about their faith. Christians instinctively want to sing to express the affection behind their words of praise, and to stir it up, knowing that words spoken flatly will not do in worship of this God.

## How Hearts Change

Since the fear of God is a matter of the heart, how you think you can cultivate it will depend on how you think our hearts work.

Take, for example, Martin Luther. He grew up believing that if you work at outward, righteous acts, you will actually become righteous. However, his experience soon proved that wrong. In fact, he found, trying to sort himself out and become righteous by his own efforts was driving him into a profoundly sinful fear and hatred of God. An outward *appearance* of righteousness he could achieve, but it would be nothing more than a hollow sham.

As Luther saw it, our sinful actions merely manifest whether we love or hate God. Simply changing our habits will not change what we love or hate. What we need is a profound change of heart, so that we want and love differently. We need the Holy Spirit to bring about a fundamental change in us, and he does this through the gospel, which preaches Christ. Only the preaching of Christ can turn a heart to fear God with loving, trembling, filial adoration. Only then, when your heart is turned toward God, will you want to fight to turn your behavior toward him.

## "Were You There When They Crucified My Lord? . . . It Causes Me to Tremble"

The cross is the most fertile soil for the fear of God. Why? First, because the cross, by the forgiveness it brings, liberates us from sinful fear. But more than that: it also cultivates the most exquisitely fearful adoration of the Redeemer. Think of the sinful woman with Jesus at the house of Simon the Pharisee: standing at Jesus's feet, "weeping, she began to wet his feet with her tears and wiped them with the hair of her head and kissed his feet and anointed them with the ointment" (Luke 7:38). At this, Jesus said to Simon:

> Do you see this woman? I entered your house; you gave me no water for my feet, but she has wet my feet with her tears and wiped them with her hair. You gave me no kiss, but from the time I came in she has not ceased to kiss my feet. You did not anoint my head with oil, but she has anointed my feet with ointment. Therefore I tell you, her sins, which are many, are forgiven—for she loved much. But he who is forgiven little, loves little. (Luke 7:44–47)

Jesus spoke of her *love*, but the intense physicality of her demonstration of affection fits Scripture's picture of *fear*. Hers was an intensely fearful love. Her love was so intense, it was fearful. When the awesome magnitude of Christ's forgiveness, the extent to which he has gone to atone for us, and therefore the terrible gravity of our sin become clear to us—as they do best at the cross—the right, loving reaction is so intense, it is fearful.

There is another reason the cross is so fertile a soil for the fear of God. For the grace of God serves as a bread-crumb trail, leading us up from the forgiveness itself to the forgiver. In the light of the cross, Christians not only thank God for his grace to us but also begin to praise him for how beautifully kind and merciful he reveals himself to be in the cross. "Oh! that a great God should be a good God," wrote John Bunyan, "a good God to an unworthy, to an undeserving, and to a people that continually do what they can to provoke the eyes of his glory; this should make us tremble."[2]

Bunyan was insistent that the most powerful change of heart toward a true fear of God comes at the foot of the cross. With striking wisdom, Bunyan wrote of how the cross simultaneously cancels the believer's guilt *and* increases our appreciation of just how vile our sinfulness is:

> For if God shall come to you indeed, and visit you with the forgiveness of sins, that visit removeth the guilt, but

increaseth the sense of thy filth, and the sense of this that God hath forgiven a filthy sinner, will make thee both rejoice and tremble. O, the blessed confusion that will then cover thy face.[3]

It is a "blessed confusion," made of sweet tears, in which God's kindness shown to you at the cross makes you weep at your wickedness. You simultaneously repent and rejoice. His mercy accentuates your wickedness, and your very wickedness accentuates his grace, leading you to a deeper and more fearfully happy adoration of the Savior.

It is not just that we marvel at the forgiveness itself. Left there we could still be full of self-love, not *enjoying* the Savior but *using* him hypocritically as the one who'll get us out of hell free. We are led from the gift to wondering at the glory of the giver, from marveling at what he has done for us to marveling at who he is in himself. His magnanimity and utter goodness undo us and fill us with a fearful and amazed adoration.

7

# The Awesome Church

NOW IS A GOOD TIME to put down this book and ask yourself
what things you fear. Our fears are highly revealing. What you
fear shows what you really love. We fear our children getting
hurt because we love them. We fear losing our jobs because we
love the security and identity they give us. We fear rejection
and criticism because we love approval. Some of these fears are
healthy, some are overblown, and some betray deeper sicknesses
in our character.

So ask yourself: What do my fears say about me and my
priorities, about what I treasure? What do they say about where
I am looking for security?

Which do you fear more: being sinful or being uncomfort-
able? God or man? *Being* a sinner or being *exposed* before others
as a sinner?

Our fears are like ECG readings, constantly telling us about the state of our hearts.

So, what does it look like when a believer is filled with a right, filial fear of God? Not a cold, dead, outward, hypocritical *show* of reverential religion, but a heartfelt quaking at the goodness and glory of the Redeemer.

## Deeper Communion with God

The fear of the Lord is a heart-level indicator of the warm communion with God that God wants with his children. It is the wondering temperament of those who have been brought to know and enjoy the everlasting mercy of God and who therefore take pleasure in him. Believers who have a right fear of the Lord will bemoan their prayerlessness but will know something of a heartfelt, affectionate prayer life. They will want to know God better and enjoy sweeter and more constant communion with him.

## Knowledge and Wisdom

"The fear of the LORD is the beginning of knowledge" (Prov. 1:7). First, the fear of the Lord brings a true knowledge of God, as Creator and as Redeemer, as majestic and as merciful. Any "knowledge of God" that is devoid of such fearful wonder is actually blind and barren. The living God is so wonderful, he is not truly known where he is not heartily adored.

But the fear of the Lord is not only the beginning of knowledge *of God*. It is also the beginning of true knowledge of ourselves. In the light of God's holiness and majesty I understand how puny, vicious, and pathetic I am. In other words, I do not have a true knowledge of myself if I do not fear God. Without that fear, my self-perception will be wildly distorted by my pride. It is when we are most thrilled with God that our masks slip and we see ourselves for what we really are: creatures, sinners, forgiven, adopted.

The fear of the Lord is also the beginning of wisdom (Prov. 9:10). But it is a very unexpected guide to wisdom. When we look for wisdom, we look to *intelligence*. We struggle to distinguish between intelligence and wisdom. Which is odd, given how the world is littered with clever fools. We need the fear of God to steer our abilities, and without it, all our abilities are a liability. Take the brilliant young theological thug online: he may just be as bright as he thinks he is, but his untempered ability only makes him more dangerous.

And therein lies a challenge for those conscious of their own ability, and a comfort for all who feel daunted by the talents of others. It is only this wonderful fear of God that can steer us wisely through life. This—not IQ—is the beginning of wisdom. Therefore, says Psalm 115:13,

he will bless those who fear the LORD,
   *both the small and the great.*

For it is not talent that God blesses so much as the fear of God.

### Becoming like God

Those who fear God become like him. For, like a fire in the heart, the fear of the Lord consumes sinful desires, and it fuels holy ones. It brings us to *adore* God and so loathe sin and long to be truly like him.

Becoming like God must mean becoming happy. God, after all, is "the blessed" or happy God (1 Tim. 1:11). You naturally expect that the fear of God would make you morose and stuffy, but quite the opposite. Unlike our sinful fears, which make us gloomy, the fear of God has a profoundly uplifting effect: it makes us happy. How can it not when it brings us to know this God?

Along with making us happy, the fear of the Lord makes believers large-hearted, like God. Think of the little story of the prophet Obadiah:

Now the famine was severe in Samaria. And Ahab called Obadiah, who was over the household. (Now Obadiah feared the LORD greatly, and when Jezebel cut off the prophets of the LORD, Obadiah took a hundred prophets and hid them

by fifties in a cave and fed them with bread and water.)
(1 Kings 18:2–4)

Far from making Obadiah self-involved and frosty, the fear of God made him generous and compassionate to those hunted prophets in need.

That large-heartedness is actually the overflow of a tender-heartedness toward God. It means that those who fear God have—to use another much-misunderstood word—a jealousy for God. Such righteous jealousy should not be confused with selfish envy: it is a love that will not let go of the beloved or make do with substitutes. As God the Father is jealous for his beloved Son, and as Christ is jealous for his bride, the church, so too those who fear God find in themselves a loving jealousy for God. Adoring him, they cannot abide his glory being diminished or stolen. False teaching will distress them, not because it contradicts their views but because it impugns *him*. Self-righteousness becomes loathsome to them because of how it steals from the glory of his grace.

From this grows another Christlike quality: humility. "So do not become proud, but fear," wrote Paul (Rom. 11:20), for trembling in wonder at God keeps one from trusting in oneself. It is the key to true humility, which is not about trying to think less of yourself or trying to think of yourself less but about marveling more at him. It is *the* antidote to pride and the prayerlessness that springs from pride. When God is so marvelous in our eyes that we rejoice and tremble, we cannot but praise him and throw ourselves on him in hearty and dependent prayer. We cannot be great in our own eyes. Not only that, but this fear levels and unites us as a church. This fear admits no boasting before God and so admits no elite and no second-class in the church. It also gathers us together in the warm and humble fellowship of a shared love.

## Finding Strength

The fear of the Lord also gives believers strength, especially in the face of anxieties and the fear of man. We don't tend to talk much about "the fear of man" today: we call it people-pleasing or peer pressure. Classic signs of it are the overcommitment that comes from an inability to say no, self-esteem issues, and an excessive sensitivity to the comments and views of others. And need I even mention our fear of evangelism?

So *how* can the fear of the Lord free us from our anxieties and our fear of man? Essentially, it acts like Aaron's staff, which ate up the staffs of the Egyptian magicians. As the fear of the Lord grows, it eclipses, consumes, and destroys all rival fears. So the Lord could advise Isaiah: "*Do not fear what they fear*, nor be in dread. But the Lord of hosts, him you shall honor as holy. *Let him be your fear*, and let him be your dread" (8:12–13). When the fear of the Lord becomes central and most important, other fears subside.

Here is truth for every Christian who needs the strength to rise above his or her anxieties, or who needs the strength to pursue an unpopular but righteous course. The fear of the Lord is the only fear that *imparts* strength. And the strength this fear gives is—uniquely—a *humble* strength. Those who fear God are simultaneously humbled *and* strengthened before his beauty and magnificence. Thus they are kept gentle and preserved from being overbearing in their strength.

All of us are temperamentally inclined to lean one way or another. Some are natural rhinos: strong and thick-skinned, but not gentle. Others are more like deer: sweet and gentle, but nervous and flighty. The fear of the Lord corrects and beautifies both temperaments, giving believers a gentle strength. It makes them—like Christ—simultaneously lamblike and lionlike.

## The Battle of Fears in the Christian Life

Since fear is a matter of the heart, reorienting our fears is no easy, quick matter. And we have an enemy whose spiteful aim is to make us afraid of God and afraid of everything, who would have us sulk and tremble. But reorienting our fears and affections is a daily battle we must join.

Left to our sinful fears of God, we will shrink from God in guilt and not enjoy his goodness. Left to our fear of man, we will wilt before every criticism, unable to enjoy real fellowship. And just as a right and happy fear of God is fostered by the truth, sinful fears grow in a bed of Satan's lies. We must counter with the truth that drives out anxiety. Into the battlefield of our troubled hearts we send the promises of God. Safe in Christ, we testify to ourselves afresh that the Almighty is our compassionate Redeemer and loving Father, and that he is able, willing, and near to us as we call on him.

In the face of our culture of anxiety, having this right fear of God will beautifully adorn and attest to the reality of the gospel we proclaim. Thereby we can give the lie to the atheist claim that liberating ourselves from the fear of God will make a less fearful culture. Quite the opposite: we can show that this fear—which is pleasurable and not disagreeable—is precisely what can liberate us from the anxieties now flooding our culture.

### Sharing God's Fearsomeness

In Song of Solomon, the bridegroom makes a statement about his bride that is eye-catching:

> You are beautiful as Tirzah, my love,
>     lovely as Jerusalem,
>     awesome as an army with banners. . . .

Who is this who looks down like the dawn,
    beautiful as the moon, bright as the sun,
    awesome as an army with banners? (6:4, 10)

The bride is like an army. And she is bright like the sun, with the reflected beauty of the moon. She has become *awesome*. That is true of the church, which is the bride of Christ: the church comes to reflect the bridegroom's awesome magnificence. We know from the apostle Paul that believers are being transformed into the image of Christ (2 Cor. 3:18). But Song of Songs specifies that that transformation is a growth in *reflected awesomeness*.

Led by the Spirit into conformity with Christ, the church begins to exhibit to the world fearsome divine qualities of holiness, happiness, wholeness, and beauty. Thus the church shines like the moon in the darkness, eliciting both wonder and dread. Believers become like heaven's Solid People in Lewis's *The Great Divorce*: their very wholeness and loving joyfulness are fearful to others. This combination is deeply alluring and inexplicable, yet at the same time troubling to unbelievers for how it exposes their grumbling crookedness. In the fear of God, believers become—like their God—blessedly and beautifully fearsome.

8

# Eternal Ecstasy

IN THE PRESENCE OF THE LORD, everyone trembles. Before him, Abraham, Joshua, David, Ezekiel, Daniel, Paul, and John all fell on their faces. But it is not just people who tremble. In Isaiah's vision of the Lord enthroned in the temple, "the foundations of the thresholds shook at the voice of him who called" (6:4). And it doesn't stop there: at his appearing,

the mountains quake before him;
the hills melt;
the earth heaves before him,
the world and all who dwell in it. (Nah. 1:5)

Just so, all things will shake and tremble at the second coming of Christ. At Sinai "his voice shook the earth, but now he has promised, 'Yet once more I will shake not only the earth but also the heavens'" (Heb. 12:26). But what sort of trembling is this that will grip the universe? For the heavens and the earth, it is clearly a trembling of exultation. The earth shakes with pleasure, for it is joining in with the joy of believers as their filial fear swells with delight at the presence of their God.

> For the creation waits with eager longing for the revealing of the sons of God. For . . . the creation itself will be set free from its bondage to corruption and obtain the freedom of the glory of the children of God. For we know that the whole creation has been groaning together in the pains of childbirth until now. (Rom. 8:19–22)

On that last day, the glory of the Lord will fill the earth, and his people will fall down in fearsome wonder, delight, and praise.

Yet, at the same appearance of the Lord in glory, the sinful fear of unbelievers will swell into a horrified dread as they hide "themselves in the caves and among the rocks of the mountains, calling to the mountains and rocks, 'Fall on us and hide us from the face of him who is seated on the throne, and from the wrath of the Lamb, for the great day of their wrath has come, and who can stand?'" (Rev. 6:15–17). Where the final appearing of the Lord in glory fills believers with an unprecedented joyful fear of the Redeemer, it fills unbelievers with a new level of dread at their Judge.

That day will usher in a new age in which both the sinful fears of unbelievers and the right fear of believers will crescendo. Both sorts of fear will climax and become eternal states—an ecstasy of terror, on the one hand, and delight, on the other.

## Hell Is a World of Fear

Hell—the destiny of all unbelievers—will be a dreadful place. Death is "the king of terrors" (Job 18:14), and hell will be the place of eternal death. It will be the ultimate sump of all sinful fears, heaving with a shared dread of holiness. There, like the demons who believe and shudder (James 2:19), its occupants will hate God and the exposing light of his glory. Sin first made the world a place full of fear, and hell is its culmination: a place of unrelieved fears, and of sinful fear come to a head.

## Heaven Is a World of Fear

Where hell is the dreadful sewer of all sinful fears, heaven is the paradise of unconfined, maximal, delighted *filial* fear. "The pillars of heaven tremble" (Job 26:11). Why? For it is the dwelling place of

> a God greatly to be feared in the council of the holy ones,
> and awesome above all who are around him. (Ps. 89:7)

And as the radiant angels now fall on their faces in fearful, ecstatic joy and adoration before God, so one day will all the saints.

## Nothing Else to Fear

Because we tend today to think of fear as a wholly negative thing, it jars us to think of fear remaining in heaven. To be sure, in heaven there will no longer be anything of which to be *afraid*. There the children of God will finally be out of reach of all danger. There will be no fear of punishment, nor any trace of any sinful fear of God left in us. We will rejoice to know him as he is, with no distortion, no misunderstanding, and no devilish whispers of doubt.

Instead, our clear apprehension of God will then enhance our wondering, trembling adoration. Not afraid of anything, the saints will be caught up into God's own fearful happiness and will be overwhelmed by exultation in the glory of God. In other words, our eternal joy will consist precisely in this fear of God: rejoicing and marveling so entirely that, like the angels, we tremble and fall on our faces in wonder.

## Like Flames of Fire

Today, we don't often speak of the emotional intensity of what our experience will be in heaven. But Scripture is clear that to be in the presence of God will give us not a tepid happiness, but a quaking, fearfully overwhelmed, ecstatic pleasure.

We get an appetizer of this heavenly and perfected filial fear in this life when we sing heartily in worship together.

> Shout to God with loud songs of joy!
> For the LORD, the Most High, is to be feared. (Ps. 47:1–2)

We catch its scent when the gospel, the Scriptures, or even some beauty in creation makes us well up or drop to our knees in sweet adoration. That overwhelmed sense when our bodies react unbidden to the strength of our affection is a small preview of the day when we will fall at our Lord's feet, too full of joy to stand.

In fact, all fears are a foretaste. The sinful fears and dreads of unbelievers are the firstfruits of hell; the filial fears of Christians are the firstfruits of heaven. Now our fears are partial; then they will be unconfined. For now, Christians see in part, and so we love and rejoice only in part. We hang our heads knowing that moments of filial, trembling wonder are all too faint and all too few. But when we see him as he is, that ecstasy will be unimpaired and absolute.

Yet, even now the Spirit is enlivening believers. From the moment of regeneration, when he breathes new life into a soul, the Spirit's work is to move us from spiritual lethargy to vivaciousness. And that is precisely all about growth in the fear of the Lord. To fear the Lord is to be more *alive*; it is for our love, joy, wonder, and worship of God to be more acute and affecting. When we rejoice in God so intensely that we quake and tremble, then are we being most heavenly.

## The Expulsive Power of a Filial Fear

Perhaps the most famous sermon ever delivered in the historic pulpit of the Tron Church in Glasgow was Thomas Chalmers's "The Expulsive Power of a New Affection." In it he argued that nobody can "dispossess the heart of an old affection, but by the expulsive power of a new one."[1] His point was that we cannot simply will ourselves to love God more; the love of sin can be expelled only by the love of God. Chalmers could have been speaking of fear, for it is the ultimate affection and the very aroma of heaven. It is the affection that expels our sinful fears and our anxieties. It is the affection that expels spiritual lethargy. To grow in this sweet and quaking wonder at God is to taste heaven now.

# Notes

*Chapter 1: Do Not Be Afraid!*

1. For a perceptive introduction to this issue, see Michael R. Emlet, "Prozac and the Promises of God: The Christian Use of Psychoactive Medication," desiringGod (website), August 22, 2019, https://www.desiringgod.org/articles/prozac-and-the-promises-of-god.

*Chapter 2: Sinful Fear*

1. Christopher Hitchens, interview on *Hannity & Colmes*, Fox News, May 13, 2007.
2. C. S. Lewis, *The Great Divorce* (London: Geoffrey Bles, 1946; repr., London: Fount, 1997), 17.
3. Lewis, *The Great Divorce*, 18.
4. Lewis, *The Great Divorce*, 46–47.

*Chapter 3: Right Fear*

1. *Scofield Reference Bible*, 1909 ed., 607n1.
2. C. H. Spurgeon, "A Fear to Be Desired," in *The Metropolitan Tabernacle Pulpit Sermons*, 63 vols. (London: Passmore & Alabaster, 1855–1917), 48:495.

3. John Bunyan, "A Treatise on the Fear of God," in *The Works of John Bunyan*, ed. George Offer, 3 vols. (Glasgow: W. G. Blackie & Son, 1854; repr., Edinburgh: Banner of Truth, 1991), 1:460–61.

4. Spurgeon, "A Fear to Be Desired," 494.

*Chapter 4: Overwhelmed by the Creator*

1. William Blake, "The Tyger" (1794).

2. Isaac Watts, "Eternal Power, Whose High Abode" (1706).

3. C. H. Spurgeon, "A Fear to Be Desired," in *The Metropolitan Tabernacle Pulpit Sermons*, 63 vols. (London: Passmore & Alabaster, 1855–1917), 48:498.

4. Spurgeon, "A Fear to Be Desired," 496.

*Chapter 5: Overwhelmed by the Father*

1. *Luther's Large Catechism* (St. Louis, MO: Concordia, 1978), 70.

2. *C. H. Spurgeon's Autobiography, Compiled from His Diary, Letters, and Records, by His Wife and His Private Secretary*, vol. 1, *1834–1854* (Chicago: Curts & Jennings, 1898), 205, my emphasis.

*Chapter 6: How to Grow in This Fear*

1. Martin Luther, *Luther's Works*, vol. 51, *Sermons I*, ed. Jaroslav Jan Pelikan, Hilton C. Oswald, and Helmut T. Lehmann (St. Louis, MO: Concordia, 1999), 139.

2. John Bunyan, "The Saints' Knowledge of Christ's Love," in *The Works of John Bunyan*, ed. George Offer, 3 vols. (Glasgow: W. G. Blackie & Son, 1854; repr., Edinburgh: Banner of Truth, 1991), 2:14.

3. John Bunyan, "A Treatise on the Fear of God," in *The Works of John Bunyan*, 1:440.

*Chapter 8: Eternal Ecstasy*

1. Thomas Chalmers, "The Expulsive Power of a New Affection," in *Posthumous Works of the Rev. Thomas Chalmers*, vol. 6 (New York: Harper & Brothers, 1848–1850), 253.

# Scripture Index

# SCRIPTURE INDEX

# Union

**We fuel reformation in churches and lives.**

Union Publishing invests in the next generation of leaders with theology that gives them a taste for a deeper knowledge of God. From books to our free online content, we are committed to producing excellent resources that will refresh, transform, and grow believers and their churches.

We want people everywhere to know, love, and enjoy God, glorifying him in everything they do. For this reason, we've collected hundreds of free articles, podcasts, book chapters, and video content for our free online collection. We also produce a fresh stream of written, audio, and video resources to help you to be more fully alive in the truth, goodness, and beauty of Jesus.

If you are hungry for reformational resources that will help you delight in God and grow in Christ, we'd love for you to visit us at unionpublishing.org.

**unionpublishing.org**

# Also Available
# from Michael Reeves

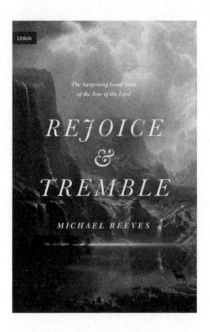

Michael Reeves brings clarity where there is confusion as he
encourages us to rejoice in the strange paradox that the gospel
both frees us from sinful fear and leads us to godly fear.

For more information, visit **crossway.org**.

"The church in the West is experiencing a lull in evangelism at a time when the need has never been greater—nor the opportunity brighter—for the church to tell the world the good news in Jesus. Daniel Hames and Michael Reeves take us to the heart of the biblical motivation to share Christ: a proper vision of our great and glorious God. The more we are overflowing with the glorious love of God, the more we will overflow with words of the gospel to others. This book will show you how to overflow with gospel love."

**Ed Stetzer,** Executive Director, Wheaton College Billy Graham Center

"I could hardly put this book down—it made my heart sing. Hames and Reeves offer immensely joyful and faith-building encouragement to all who love and long to enjoy and participate in God's mission."

**Gloria Furman,** coeditor, *Joyfully Spreading the Word*; author, *Missional Motherhood*

"After decades of mission work, I've witnessed the various motivations driving missionary efforts, from the worst (a guilty conscience or vain ambition) to the good (a genuine concern for the lost). But Hames and Reeves call us to remember the best: that knowing and loving God deeply, fully, with a reckless abandon is our first and most essential priority for missions. They make it clear that when we truly know the nature of our loving, giving, gracious God, when we delight in him, we have the true fuel from God for missions. Don't let anyone you know go to the mission field without reading this book."

**J. Mack Stiles,** former Pastor, Erbil Baptist Church, Iraq

"The big idea of this book is both simple and life-transforming: 'It is precisely *because* God is outgoing and communicative that he is so good and delightful.' Thus, as this God's beloved people delight in him, they are propelled to speak about his goodness to others by communicating the good news. Yes, evangelism is a biblically commanded duty for all Christians. Yes, the Great Commission is a scripturally grounded purpose of the church. Yes, missions is a theologically supported enterprise for the benefit of the world. Ultimately, however, this endeavor is an overflow from knowing God. This book gets this truth right!"

**Gregg R. Allison,** Professor of Christian Theology, The Southern Baptist Theological Seminary; Secretary, Evangelical Theological Society; author, *Historical Theology*; *Sojourners and Strangers*; and *Embodied*

"Missiology tends to be long on pragmatics and short on theology. What a mistake! This book grounds our missiology in our theology, and provides a vision for how the truths of the Bible shape us and authentically motivate us toward the Great Commission."

**Josh Moody,** Senior Pastor, College Church, Wheaton, Illinois; President and Founder, God Centered Life Ministries

*WHAT FUELS THE*
*MISSION OF THE CHURCH?*

# WHAT FUELS THE MISSION OF THE CHURCH?

*DANIEL HAMES AND MICHAEL REEVES*

**CROSSWAY**®

WHEATON, ILLINOIS

Trade paperback ISBN: 978-1-4335-7518-1
ePub ISBN: 978-1-4335-7521-1
PDF ISBN: 978-1-4335-7519-8
Mobipocket ISBN: 978-1-4335-7520-4

---

### Library of Congress Cataloging-in-Publication Data

Names: Hames, Daniel, author. | Reeves, Michael (Michael Richard Ewert), author.
Title: What fuels the mission of the church? / Daniel Hames and Michael Reeves.
Other titles: God shines forth
Description: Wheaton, Illinois : Crossway, 2022. | Series: Union | Includes bibliographical references and index.
Identifiers: LCCN 2022005084 (print) | LCCN 2022005085 (ebook) | ISBN 9781433575181 (trade paperback) | ISBN 9781433575198 (pdf) | ISBN 9781433575204 (mobipocket) | ISBN 9781433575211 (epub)
Subjects: LCSH: Spirituality—Christianity. | Mission of the church. | Missions—Theory.
Classification: LCC BV4501.3 .H3535 2022b (print) | LCC BV4501.3 (ebook) | DDC 248—dc23/eng/20220528
LC record available at https://lccn.loc.gov/2022005084
LC ebook record available at https://lccn.loc.gov/2022005085

---

Crossway is a publishing ministry of Good News Publishers.

| VP | | 31 | 30 | 29 | 28 | 27 | 26 | 25 | 24 | 23 | 22 |
|----|----|----|----|----|----|----|----|----|----|----|----|
| 15 | 14 | 13 | 12 | 11 | 10 | 9 | 8 | 7 | 6 | 5 | 4 | 3 | 2 | 1 |

*For Paul and Janey Hames*
*Psalm 113*

# Contents

# Series Preface

OUR INNER CONVICTIONS AND VALUES shape our lives and our ministries. And at Union—the cooperative ministries of Union School of Theology, Union Publishing, Union Research, and Union Mission (visit www.theolo.gy)—we long to grow and support men and women who will delight in God, grow in Christ, serve the church, and bless the world. This Union series of books is an attempt to express and share those values.

They are values that flow from the beauty and grace of God. The living God is so glorious and kind, he cannot be known without being adored. Those who truly know him will love him, and without that heartfelt delight in God, we are nothing but hollow hypocrites. That adoration of God necessarily works itself out in a desire to grow in Christlikeness. It also fuels a love for Christ's precious bride, the church, and a desire humbly to serve—rather than use—her. And, lastly, loving God brings us to share his concerns, especially to see his life-giving glory fill the earth.

Each exploration of a subject in the Union series will appear in two versions: a full volume and a concise one. The concise treatments, such as this one, are like shorter guided tours: they stick to the main streets and move on fast. You may find, at the end of this little book, that you have questions or want to explore some more: in that case, the fuller volume will take you further up and further in.

My hope and prayer is that these books will bless you and your church as you develop a deeper delight in God that overflows in joyful integrity, humility, Christlikeness, love for the church, and a passion to make disciples of all nations.

*Michael Reeves*
SERIES EDITOR

# Introduction

## The Great Admission

LET'S GET IT OUT IN THE OPEN right at the beginning. Doesn't something about mission and evangelism just feel "off" to you? Every Christian knows we're meant to share the gospel and look for opportunities to witness to Christ, yet almost all of us find it a genuine struggle, if not a gloomy discouragement. The vital, final thing Jesus left his followers to do—the Great Commission!—seems to be the one thing about the Christian life that, frankly, doesn't feel so great. While we've heard the motivational sermons, sat in the "how to" seminars, and tried to crank ourselves up to initiating a deep conversation with friends or colleagues, we're often left feeling awkward and ashamed.

Complicating matters is that most of us *do* have a sincere desire that the people we love would come to know the Lord as we do. It's just that this longing doesn't seem to translate very easily or very often into actual evangelism. Any passion and boldness we may have in prayer apparently evaporates under the spotlight at the dinner table or on the coffee break. Our words dry up, our confidence deserts us, and we could wish we were almost anywhere else in the world.

If this all sounds familiar to you, you are not alone. So, what is going on? What is the mysterious cause of our complicated relationship with mission?

Perhaps insecurity keeps us from evangelism. We worry what other people might think of us if we start "Bible-thumping," so we keep quiet. Perhaps our problem is fear of failure. We don't feel well enough equipped or aren't confident enough in the power of the gospel, so we dare not risk rejection or (perhaps worse) indifference. These things may play a part in our predicament, but the diagnosis doesn't quite fit the symptoms. Personal insecurity or fear of failure seems to presuppose a burning passion in us to share the gospel that is simply being inhibited by some external barriers needing to be removed. A little training or a good pep talk could have us out on the streets in no time, fulfilling our hearts' desire to proclaim Christ every moment of every day!

But here is the great admission that many of us need to make: when it comes to the Great Commission, our *hearts* aren't really in it. Something far deeper than practical limitations is causing our mission fatigue.

## Here's the Catch

If we are entirely honest, when we think about evangelism, we often feel something close to resentment. Many of us silently grumble that, in being recruited to evangelism, we're being put upon. We first came to know Jesus very happily, receiving his mercy and his invitation to new life, but then along came this unexpected and slightly puzzling additional step of having to be a witness to him in the world. Like a car shifting into the wrong gear, we came to a juddering halt. We'd been *offered* free grace and forgiveness, but now there's a *demand*? Christianity, we fear, was just too good to be true. Mission is the inevitable catch tacked on to the list of benefits we signed up for. It's the complicated, unwelcome add-on to salvation that God has included in the deal as the sweetener for himself.

But it seems that the Christian is left with no choice. In light of everything God has done for us, we owe him—and this is what he's stipulated. Having been drawn in by promises of easy yokes and light burdens, we have the sensation of being trapped in a contractual obligation. The thought of enjoying God forever had sounded warm and inviting, but the very word *evangelism* can send a chill down the spine. The worst of it is that all this ultimately reflects very badly on God, who begins not to look so good and attractive as we first thought. Like a PR agency representing a difficult client, we begin to wonder what we've got ourselves into. This reveals the real issue. The problem at the root of all our struggles with mission is almost certainly right at the beginning: with our view of God.

## Getting God Right

If we believe that God is simply out to impose himself on the world and suck it dry of glory and praise, then we will never love and want to share him (even if we tell ourselves that God is entitled to do whatever he wants). If God seems to us a demanding taskmaster, we will never be his eager ambassadors in the world. If we feel ourselves conned into having to perform evangelism, we will never warm to the calling he has set before us. Unless we honestly find God to be beautiful and enjoyable, we'll have nothing worth saying to the people around us.

So this book is an invitation to start again at the beginning with your vision of God. Our aim is to set before your eyes God as he truly is: God who is so full of life and goodness that he loves to be known; not as a campaign to *impose* himself on us or on the world but to *give* himself and *share* his own life with the world. We want to show that the God of mission is no different from the God of the gospel. In fact, it is precisely *because* God is outgoing and communicative that he is so good and delightful. His natural fullness and superabundance mean that he does not need to *take* or *demand* from us but freely and kindly loves to *bless* us. His mission is not to wring out the world for every last drop but to *fill* it with his own divine joy and beauty. Seeing *this* glorious God will change everything for us.

Mission is no clunky add-on to your own delighting in God. Instead, it is the natural overflow and expression of the enjoyment you have of him so that, *like him*, you gladly go out to fill the world with the word of his goodness.

Our going out to the world with the gospel is not an endeavor that Christians have to hitch on to knowing God, bringing to the task a vigor and vim outsourced from elsewhere. Rather, the reality of God is itself at once all the motivation, the content, and the zest of our going. It is precisely because God, from his own glorious fullness, fills us with joy in him that we begin to bubble over with it to those around. The wellspring of healthy, happy mission is God himself.

1

# The Glory of God

HAPPY MISSION PRESUPPOSES HAPPY CHRISTIANS.

There is a kind of mission that can be carried out by miserable Christians, and though it may be doctrinally correct and carefully organized, it will only reflect the emptiness in their own hearts. Christians who don't *enjoy* God can't and won't wholeheartedly commend him to others. If we fear that God's love for us is reluctant or that his approval rests on our performance, we won't feel any real affection for him, our service will be grudging, and the world will likely see through us.

At the heart of happy Christianity is knowing God rightly, which means beginning all our thinking with Jesus Christ.

## Step into the Light

Jesus says, "All things have been handed over to me by my Father, and no one knows the Son except the Father, and no one knows the Father except the Son and anyone to whom the Son chooses to reveal him" (Matt. 11:27). The truth of God is naturally hidden from the world in the closed loop of relationship between the Father and the Son, and none of us can guess our way in. Only the Son, the one who knows the Father, can open this knowledge to us. Anyone can come to know the living God and find rest in him, but it is uniquely to *Jesus* they must come.

John calls Jesus "the true *light*, which gives light to everyone" (John 1:9). Here we meet a very common scriptural theme: that of the Son *enlightening* us. Paul does the same in 2 Corinthians 4 when he speaks of "the *light* of the gospel of the glory of Christ, who is the image of God" (v. 4). Indeed, he writes that "God, who said, 'Let light shine out of darkness,' has *shone in our hearts* to give the light of the knowledge of the glory of God *in the face of Jesus Christ*" (v. 6).

Time and again, Scripture is clear that sinful humanity languishes in unknowing darkness, but that the work of Jesus is to be the light in the dark rooms of our hearts and minds, showing us the Father.

### Source and Beam

Since Jesus *is* himself God—the eternal Son of the Father—he is God *with* us. Not an expert lecturer or detailed commentator we may learn from, but God in person, reaching out to us to be known by us.

The writer to the Hebrews describes Jesus as the "exact imprint" or perfect representation of God to us, and also "the radiance of the glory of God" (1:3). To speak of Jesus as the "radiance" of God's glory is to say that Jesus is not a light directed at some *other* subject, like a flashlight pointed at your shoes in a tent at night. Radiance, like the sun and its beams, speaks of something—or someone—that, by nature, shines out and *gives* light. In other words, it is not that God is hiding in the dark and we must enlist Jesus to help us seek him out. Rather, God himself *is* the source of that light that comes to us in Christ. Put another way, the light that shines on us in Jesus *is* the light of the Father. The Father and the Son are one being, one God. The eternal life of God *is* the Father begetting his Son in the Holy Spirit. What we see in Jesus is not peripheral to the being of God. No, the Father, radiating his Son, shines like the sun in the sky and, by those beams, communicates himself to us.

In the radiance of Jesus, we not only are learning something *about* God but are *receiving God himself.*

## Jesus, the Glory of God

Jesus *is* the glory of God: the very outshining radiance of his being.

Scripturally, glory has to do with the "weight" or "copiousness" of something—its sheer, unmissable presence, especially in bright, shining splendor. For Jesus Christ to be the "radiance of the glory of God" is for him to be the weight or the substance of God impressed upon us, beaming on us, *given* to us.

When John went with Peter and James up the mountain and saw the Lord transfigured (Matt. 17:1–5), amid all the brightness and light, what is trumpeted most clearly is the Father's complete approval of his Son. Nothing and nobody else could more completely unveil, display, and thus please God the Father. In Jesus, we see the very being of God shining forth on us. He shows us a God who is fundamentally outgoing, outshining, and self-giving. He wants to be known by us, to be with us, even possessed by us, so that we will call him *our* God (Jer. 31:33).

### Mission's Motor

If someone were to ask us, "What is God like?" the answer must be "Jesus Christ." And this is the beating heart of mission.

God's glory—his own naturally overspilling life, seen in his Son—is mission's *rationale* and its motor. In whatever sense mission is about our going out into the world to make God known, it is only ever our being caught up in the already gushing tide of blessing that flows from the heart of the Father in the Son.

Those who bask in the sunshine of this loving and generous God are the happiest Christians and the happiest missionaries. Seeing in Jesus what our God is really like causes us to shine like him. We come to share his great heart's desire that his love, goodness, and righteousness would bless all the world.

But we haven't said all that must be said about the glory of God. We haven't yet said everything that must be said about Jesus. There is a strange but brighter brightness we still need to unveil: his death for us.

2

# The Lamb on His Throne

CHRISTIANS SPEAK QUITE A BIT about God's glory, but we don't always do so in a thoroughly *Christian* way. We treat glory as though its meaning were self-evident and self-explanatory, allowing our natural, human idea of glory to lead the charge in our imaginations. In our fallen thinking, for God to be glorious is simply for him to be *great*.

But when we begin to see Jesus himself as the Glory of the Father and let him shape our idea of glory, we find that God is far better than we ever dared to believe, and his glory, beautifully different from our own. Nowhere is this more sharply detailed—and nowhere is the glory of God more tightly defined in Scripture—than on the cross of Jesus.

### In the Throne Room

In the book of Revelation, the apostle John has a glimpse behind the curtain of the cosmos. As he looks into the great spiritual realities of the heavenly realm, he sees a throne (Rev. 4:3). The living God is seated there, and in his hand is a sealed scroll (Rev. 5:1). This scroll, we learn through the book, contains the meaning of history and the great arc of the purposes of God in it all, and nobody can open it and unlock its mysteries except "the Lion of the Tribe of Judah" (Rev. 5:5). Yet, as John watches, he sees not a roaring lion, but "a Lamb standing, as though it had been slain" (Rev. 5:6). The Lamb takes the scroll and opens the seals, and the company of heaven sings to him,

> Worthy are you to take the scroll
>> and to open its seals,
> for you were slain, and by your blood you ransomed
>> people for God
>> from every tribe and language and people and nation.
>> (Rev. 5:9)

Here is the most surprising and counterintuitive message. We would never have expected the God of glory and all his purposes to be revealed *this* way: in death. Yet *the Lamb who was slain* is specifically presented as the key to understanding it all.

Paul writes that the cross is the point at which God slices into our human ways of thinking—so thoroughly distorted and polluted by sin—to confront us and contradict us. Our natural assumption is that the crucifixion of the Son of God would be "folly" (1 Cor. 1:18), when in fact it is "the power of God and the wisdom of God" displayed (1 Cor. 1:24). If we want to know the true power and wisdom of God, then it is to the cross we must look.

## Blood and Glory

So how are we to relate the glory of God to the cross? If Christ is the radiance of God's glory, is the crucifixion not the Glory of God himself being snuffed out? This is an important question, because many of us see the grace and mercy on display in Jesus's death for us but fear it was nothing more than an episode of atypical friendliness in God. Wonderfully, John's Gospel speaks of Jesus's death *as his glory*.

In John 2, Jesus attends the wedding in Cana where the wine runs out. When his mother, Mary, asks him to step in and help, he puzzlingly replies, "My hour has not yet come" (v. 4). Nevertheless, he turns water into wine, to the delight of the wedding guests, and John notes, "This, the first of his signs, Jesus did at Cana in Galilee, and manifested his glory" (v. 11). This sets up questions that hang over the rest of his Gospel. When will be the "hour" or moment to which Jesus is referring? What is the "glory" he is manifesting?

When Jesus enters the city of Jerusalem in John 12, everything falls into place at once. He says that, at long last, "the hour has come for the Son of Man to be glorified" (v. 23). Immediately he prays to his Father: "Now is my soul troubled. And what shall I say? 'Father, save me from this hour'? But for this purpose I have come to this hour. Father, glorify your name" (vv. 27–28). Then he speaks of being "lifted up from the earth" to "show by what kind of death he was going to die" (vv. 32–33).

The hour of Jesus's glorification is nothing other than the soul-troubling death that lies before him. The glory—the weight and substance of *who he is*—is to be set out for all to see on the cross. This was his purpose from the beginning, and not only his glorification but the Father's glorification *in him*. Jesus considers the "hour" in which he is hoisted up in shame and agony on the tree to be the moment of his glory and of his Father's great pleasure in him. Could it be that, in the horror of Golgotha, we see played out before us the *love and glory* of the Father and Son? That God shows us most deeply and wonderfully who he is in this sacrifice of himself?

The Roman soldiers cannot have known the truth they were preaching as they mockingly laid on him the purple robe and crown of thorns, fixing to his cross the sign "the King of the Jews." For here was the King of the universe bearing in himself all the curse (Gen. 3:18); the Lamb taking up his throne. Against all our fears, the cross was not a detour for God the Son. It was and is his glory. It is his glory that his soul should be troubled so that ours need not be (John 12:27; 14:1), that he himself should go down into the grave to bear the fruit of our eternal life (John 12:24), that he should be crucified between two thieves, "numbered with the transgressors" (Isa. 53:12), in the fate that should have been ours. As the eternal one empties himself into history and his love is poured out in blood, just as the festal wine has been, we can only stand amazed and say, with Thomas, "My Lord and my God!" (John 20:28).

## Who Is Like the Lord Our God?

The cross is glory in that God shows himself there decisively. The cross is the glorification of *the* Glory (the Son!) of God. It stands as the defining moment in God's relationship to all creation—the pinnacle and epitome of all he desires to show us of himself.

Doing theology from the cross is like going through the looking glass with Alice into a totally different way of seeing everything. In fact, it is a death-and-resurrection experience for us, as "the Lord kills and brings to life" (1 Sam. 2:6). The air on the other side is different, and there is a freshness and beauty that we never sensed before. No matter how we might have thought of God before, at the cross, we learn that God truly *loves* us sinners and has done everything necessary to redeem us and bring us to himself.

The revelation of God at the cross torpedoes our expectations of him. Where we have imagined him to be distant and severe, the cross says, "God so loved the world, that he gave his only Son" (John 3:16). Where we have imagined him demanding a perfection we cannot offer, the cross says, "God shows his love for us in that while we were still sinners, Christ died for us" (Rom. 5:8). Where we have imagined ourselves dropping out of God's favor by our frequent disobedience, the cross says: "If anyone does sin, we have an advocate with the Father, Jesus Christ the righteous. He is the propitiation for our sins" (1 John 2:1–2). This way, the cross kindly puts us to death, contradicting us in every way, totally upending our human ways of thinking. All this is completely beautiful to us as we sing with the psalmist,

Who is like the LORD our God,
    who is seated on high,
who looks far down
    on the heavens and the earth? (Ps. 113:5–6)

3

# Fullness

If Jesus truly is the radiance of the Father, then all the goodness we see demonstrated and enacted in Christ's living, dying, and rising flows from God's own eternal life and being.

## I Am Who I Am

In Exodus 3, Moses meets the Lord at the burning bush and asks him, "What is your name?" The Lord answers, "I AM WHO I AM. . . . Say this to the people of Israel: 'I AM has sent me to you'" (v. 14). God has answered Moses with a sentence. But then he says, "*The LORD*, the God of your fathers, the God of Abraham, the God of Isaac, and the God of Jacob, has sent me to you" (v. 15). These two parallel answers are related. The name "LORD" in our Bibles stands in for the personal name of God, which, in

31

turn, comes from the word for "I am." When we speak of "the LORD," we are, in effect, calling God "the One Who Is," for he does not receive his name, identity, or existence from anyone or anything else: the life of God is self-contained and self-sustaining. He does not depend on anything to be who he is: he simply and eternally *is*. God does not rely on anything outside himself, and he does not evolve or improve. Having fullness of being, how could he? God's eternal life is unbeatably perfect as it is.

This is God—Father, Son, and Spirit—before, beyond, and above all created things. Yet the triune life is not a fortress, shut up against the world. No, the very life of God—all that he is in himself—overflows.

## The Infinite Happiness of God

God the Father has eternally given to his Son. "For as the Father has life in himself," Jesus says, "so he has granted the Son also to have life in himself" (John 5:26). The eternal life of God *is* the Father begetting his Son in the Holy Spirit. The nature and quality of this eternal life is revealed to us when, on the night of his arrest, Jesus prays, "Father . . . you *loved* me before the foundation of the world" (John 17:24).

The Father's default way of being is to be filled with pleasure in fellowship with his Son in the Spirit. This love is ground zero of all the blessings that spill out on us in the creation of the world and in the gospel. God's being in eternal, self-sufficient life is no departure from the goodness of Jesus. It is the very fountainhead of his—and our—happiness. From the fellowship of Father, Son, and Spirit, superabundant goodness *spreads*.

## Say No to Needy Gods

The glorious fullness of the living God revealed in Jesus sets him apart from all other gods. Throughout the Old Testament, the idols that tempt the Israelites are constantly described as "empty," and they hollow out those who worship them. They require the shedding of human blood (1 Kings 18:28) and the sacrifice of precious children (2 Kings 23:10); they cannot bring the rain (Jer. 14:22); and while they gladly take offerings, they cannot save in the times of trouble (Jer. 11:12).

In Acts 19:28, when Paul has preached the gospel in Ephesus, Demetrius the idol maker complains that the "great goddess" Artemis will be "counted as nothing" if Paul wins converts. This is quite an admission! Artemis is "nothing" without her temple and her worshipers, who could leave her at any moment.

All false gods *need* worship and service and sustenance. Not being self-existent or full in themselves, they demand, consume, and are never satisfied. Like hungry and irritable toddlers, they tend to throw tantrums and strike fear into their devotees. They are never satisfied and must always be on the take. Meanwhile, nothing about our God is withdrawn or protective, as though he were lacking or needy. He alone is eternally good, loving, and full of life. It is his very nature to abound, to give, and to radiate.

## You Open Your Hand

God's fullness sets him apart not only from idols but also from us creatures. Humanity is, by nature, dependent and needy. Not only do we receive our life in the first place (unlike the Lord), but also we need to eat, drink, and sleep in order for that life to continue. God, who has life in himself, must *bestow* it on us, and God, who is eternal, must *preserve* us in that life.

Every time we hungrily sit down to a meal or collapse into bed, we are confronted with our own limits and finitude—our need to take something in before we can begin to give out again. It is no accident that we are this way.

You are created to desire and crave—and to have poured into you from outside—life and sustenance, whether physical or spiritual. The Lord has made us this way to show that he alone is the source of life and that we must go to him for it. Our very nature as human beings is to be contingent, always looking to our ever-giving God for life and everything.

> The eyes of all look to you,
>> and you give them food in due season.

You open your hand;

>  you satisfy the desire of every living thing.
>>  (Ps. 145:15–16)

## Full and Empty Living

For too many of us, our experience of the Christian life and of mission feels as though it is running on empty. Our view of God has slowly become distorted and skewed, so we do not set out filled with joy and satisfaction in him. In our efforts to serve a demanding god of our imaginations, our discipleship and evangelism feel eked out, because they are not fueled by an all-generous, giving God. If our God is not full, neither will we be.

But when we come to look at God in the light of Christ, we see that our God is an eternal spring of happiness and goodness, completely and irrepressibly *full*—full of glory, full of life, and full of blessing for the world. He is no black hole, eternally swallowing up glory, but an everlasting sun, *radiating* glory to the farthest reaches of our darkness. In Christ, God beams upon us, reveals his goodness, and shares himself with us. His happy fullness—and our derived enjoyment of him—is the heartbeat of mission, too.

4

# Emptiness

IF GOD IS REALLY SO GOOD, surely mission must be the easiest work in the world. Simply hold out Jesus in his gospel, and people should come flocking.

Of course, that's not how it is. Quite the opposite. Bizarrely, the wonderful good news of free grace is a tough sell. People dislike not just the idea of God in general but the message of the gospel specifically. Human beings are fallen, and this is why we do not intuitively worship, trust, and love God. The radiance of God's glory shines not into neutrality but into *darkness*. The truth is that human beings, originally made in the image of God to love and enjoy him, reflecting his radiance in the world, have become *in*glorious through turning away from him.

## Made for Glory

We were created to live in the presence and blessing of God. The first couple, Adam and Eve, were placed in the paradise of Eden, which God himself had planted for them, and where they were to enjoy fellowship with him. From the garden, they were to rule over the creation, multiplying to fill it (Gen. 1:28; 2:8).

Paul writes that Adam was a "type," or pattern, of Christ, "the one who was to come" (Rom. 5:14), because his purpose was to picture the one man who has always enjoyed the love of his Father (John 17:24), to whom every knee would one day bow (Phil. 2:10), and who would come to fill all things (Eph. 1:23). Here is the root of our sense of dignity, the reason we feel an itch for purpose and significance. We were created *for* glory and to *be* glorious, like our God.

## Enslaved to Emptiness

Sin unraveled all this. More than simply disobeying a command and getting himself into trouble, Adam in his fall turned away from the Lord, the fountain of all life and love. The aftermath was devastating, for in denying God, Adam also defaced himself, enslaving himself and all his children to emptiness.

"Man is like a breath [literally, "emptiness"]," says David; "his days are like a passing shadow" (Ps. 144:4). It is now impossible for us to imagine life and humanity before the fall of Adam.

Like a laptop computer with the power cord unplugged, even the life we appear to hold within us is gradually ebbing away. Disconnected from the ever-full source of life and light and love, we are but waning shadows of all we were intended to be.

All flesh is grass,
>    and all its beauty is like the flower of the field.
The grass withers, the flower fades
>    when the breath of the LORD blows on it;
>    surely the people are grass.
The grass withers, the flower fades
>    but the word of our God will stand forever.
>        (Isa. 40:6–8)

## The Image Defaced

Our fallen emptiness means we cannot be radiant as we were meant to be. When, in the fall, Adam ceased to look to God and looked instead to himself (even to his own body in its nakedness and vulnerability, Gen. 3:7), the crucial bond between the divine image and the image bearer was broken. The image of God in humanity was defaced, and the glory dimmed.

Adam's loss of glory became the family trait. As well as being infected with his guilt and his death, each of bears his likeness in behavior, "for all have sinned and fall short of the glory of

God" (Rom. 3:23). It would be wrong to say that fallen people no longer bear the image of God at all: sin has not entirely destroyed all that God created. Nevertheless, the image is spoiled and marred such that we do not shine out with the glory of God.

With our eyes off God in his glory and forever flitting about in the darkest corners, we are gradually formed into the image of creatures that deprive us of the life we miss and cannot satisfy us or restore us to our proper place. However frustrated and unfulfilled we find ourselves, we nevertheless settle into unhappy cycles of worshiping nothingness, with nothing to gain and nothing to give out.

This lies behind what can feel like the most perplexing response we encounter in evangelism: apathy. This reaction may frustrate the evangelist, but it should provoke our compassion. It is the fruit of a heart that is simultaneously deeply unsatisfied and without hope of satisfaction. The emptiness of sin is so profound that it leaves us hardened and stagnant.

### Mirror, Mirror, on the Wall . . .

Given all we have seen, it is no wonder that our culture is overrun with issues surrounding identity. Since the garden, we do not participate in the fullness of God's life, his image in us has been vandalized, and we are consumed with self-love. Sinners do not know who, why, or what they are. Many people want to improve themselves but simply do not know what "mended" or whole people would look like. Sensing our brokenness, we make wild stabs at solutions: political activism, radical moral codes, mindfulness, self-improvement, dieting fads, and so on.

Feeling our emptiness, we crave the praise and attention of other people, making ourselves hostage to their opinions. We may find ourselves emotionally leaning on others too heavily, forcing friendships or romantic relationships to carry a weight of expectation they are unable to bear. Anxiety, stress, depression, and loneliness soon follow.

The emptiness and darkness of this present age form the context and backdrop of the mission of the church (Titus 2:12). They mark the condition of the people around us who must hear the gospel of the glory of God if they are to be set free. The church alone can show the world where real fullness, happiness, and life are to be found.

5

# Born in Zion

WHAT WAS GOD TO DO WITH HUMANITY, lost in this darkness and futility? God *reached out*. Christ came to *remake* us after his image.

This is where our mission began. For this renewal of human beings is not only the birth of *Christians* but the birth of *missionaries*, as we who once were darkness become "light in the Lord" (Eph. 5:8).

When the psalmist applauds the glory of Zion in Psalm 87, he includes a surprising list of inhabitants: Rahab, Babylon, Philistia, Tyre, and Cush (v. 4). These are Gentile outsiders being counted as residents of Zion, included with Israel, fully belonging as though they were born in the city of God. The psalmist says of each, "This one was born there" in Zion (v. 4). By God's grace, out of Rahab and Babylon, from darkness and nothingness, new life is found and a new identity is established. Those who once were far off have been brought near to share in the call to proclaim the gospel in the world (Eph. 2:11–13).

## The Image Restored

In Adam, humanity had slipped far from its noble purpose in creation, leaking life, falling short of God's glory, and turning in on itself in idolatry and selfishness. But Jesus Christ came into the world to turn us around.

Every moment of Jesus's life on earth was a display of humanity as it was always supposed to be. For the first time, a human being lived in the fullness of God's intentions for us. He perfectly loved, trusted, and obeyed his Father (John 14:31) and poured out his heart to him in prayer (Luke 6:12), even though he faced all the same temptation, weakness, and suffering we do (Heb. 2:18; 4:15). He was morally faultless himself but never lacked compassion for even the most notorious sinners (Mark 2:15–17). He exercised rule over the creation, stilling wind and waves (Matt. 8:27) and driving out the corruption of demons and diseases (Matt. 12:22–24). He amazed his disciples with words of truth that could only be God's own self-expression (Mark 10:24). He went silently to his death, giving himself in love for those who hated him (Mark 15:5). Full of life, gloriously good, and overflowing with kindness, Jesus was everything a human being is *meant* to be—the definitive likeness of God, revealed in the original image himself. Here, at last, was a real man.

## The Great Exchange

Christ came not merely to set us an example to follow but also to take hold of humanity, binding himself to us and us to himself. He came to take the old humanity to the cross with him and put it to death, raising us with him in his resurrection. "Father," he prayed shortly before his crucifixion, "I desire that they also, whom you have given me, *may be with me where I am*" (John 17:24). Salvation is an exchange. He came into the wreckage of humanity, taking all our sin and death to himself on the cross, and he raised us to the fellowship with the Father that he himself eternally had.

Now, Christ's perfect life and righteousness are credited to us (2 Cor. 5:21), his resurrection is the guarantee of our own to come (Rom. 6:5), and we receive a whole catalog of spiritual blessings in and through him (Eph. 1:3–14).

## You Have Been Filled in Him

On the other side of the cross, this redeemed human life is the "new self, which is being renewed in knowledge after the image of its creator" (Col. 3:10). The same Spirit who filled, led, and empowered Jesus (Matt. 12:28; Luke 4:1) now dwells in us (Eph. 2:22).

When the Colossian church was facing pressure to turn aside from Jesus to various extraneous spiritual practices, Paul wrote to reassure them of the complete sufficiency of Jesus and the life they already had in him:

> See to it that no one takes you captive by philosophy and empty deceit, according to human tradition, according to the elemental spirits of the world, and not according to Christ. *For in him the whole fullness of deity dwells bodily, and you have been filled in him.* (Col. 2:8—10)

With Jesus, we who naturally have nothing are given everything. Empty, hollow sinners are enriched, ennobled, and *filled* as we are united with the one who has in himself the fullness of God.

## "Hearts Unfold like Flowers before Thee"

When we come to the cross of Christ and are filled by him, the first change we experience is in our relationship with God. We find ourselves increasingly warming with his love, unclenching our fists, and coming freely to adore and enjoy him. Unconsciously forgetting ourselves, we can sing,

Joyful, joyful, we adore Thee,
God of glory, Lord of love;
Hearts unfold like flowers before Thee,
opening to the sun above.[1]

Finding this treasure outside ourselves, we become refreshingly un-self-obsessed. Once, we cringed and retreated before the light, but now we are blossoming flowers, soaking up the sunshine. In humble, happy Christians, the glory of God is echoed back to him in gratitude. Now, turned inside out by the gospel of Jesus, we look out from ourselves toward God in worship. But there is a second opening up we experience too. We radiate outward into the world.

## A Glorious Image

When empty ones are filled by the God of fullness, we become bright and glorious like him, for "we all, with unveiled face, beholding the glory of the Lord, are being transformed into the *same image* from *one degree of glory to another*" (2 Cor. 3:18). Christians take on Jesus's radiance.

Here is the birth of our mission, for the Christian's new birth is a birth into a life in the image of the God who is always on mission. Now born in Zion, we belong to the Lord and manifest his life in our own lives. Because this life is *his* gift—the gift of the ever-outgoing, generous God—it is a *godly* life that delights to multiply, spread out, and increase. So believers become shining lights in the world, as he is *the* light of the world (Matt. 5:16; John 8:12), shining with his own light as we hold him out to "a crooked and twisted generation" (Phil. 2:14–16).

## Cross-Shaped Living

Just as the cross reveals God to be full and glorious in love, humility, and blessing, so it creates Christians who are the same way. Happiness, beauty, and humility flow from the lives of those who are restored in *the* image of God. This transformation from our empty, fallen life to the glorious, truly human (Christlike!) life is at the heart of healthy mission. The cross makes mean souls into lavish souls.

The glory of the Christian is always Jesus Christ and him crucified. "Far be it from me to boast except in the cross of our Lord Jesus Christ," says Paul (Gal. 6:14). Knowing that we are empty ones, now full of him, we always place Jesus himself at the foreground rather than ourselves. It is Jesus we have to offer to the world.

6

# Arise, Shine!

IF CHRISTIANS ARE RENEWED in the image of God, "born in Zion," and shining with the glory of the Lord, why does mission continue to be such a challenge for us?

Too often, we find ourselves fragile and timid in mission, propelled by a mixed bag of motivations and emotions. We may be totally committed to mission as an activity of the church but feel low on energy and enthusiasm. We know that despite everything being right in theory, something is still missing, and we are simply not sparkling with the beauty and goodness of Jesus. While we know God to be full, our mission feels empty. What is going on?

## How to Be a Bad Missionary

Jesus reproved the religious leaders of his day for a distortion of mission that was not the fruit of happy hearts but the toil of spiritual captives.

But woe to you, scribes and Pharisees, hypocrites! For you shut the kingdom of heaven in people's faces. For you neither enter yourselves nor allow those who would enter to go in. Woe to you, scribes and Pharisees, hypocrites! For you travel across sea and land to make a single proselyte, and when he becomes a proselyte, you make him twice as much a child of hell as yourselves. (Matt. 23:13–15)

The scribes and Pharisees belonged not to the kingdom of heaven but to hell, and they willingly went great distances for their "mission." Notice that Jesus referred to their fruit not as "converts" but as "proselytes." Self-justifying, empire-building evangelists may see many proselytes won by force of personality or impressive communication, but hypocrites can only give birth to hypocrites.

This is the very definition of "empty" mission—and it begins with a tragically thin view of God. Driven by the glory of people rather than of God (John 5:44), the Pharisees were insecure and petty (Matt. 12:2), willing to climb over others for attention, praying ostentatiously in public places, and comparing themselves with one another (Matt. 6:5; Luke 18:11). Pharisees cannot truly love God or other people, because they have not first enjoyed the love of God for themselves. When disciples of an empty, demanding god do mission, they will tend to be results-driven bullies. Even an evangelist who *preaches* a gospel of grace but is really justifying himself betrays the fact that God seems to him neither near nor kind—not truly gracious or glorious.

## Sticks and Carrots

When Christians are not filled to overflowing with the glorious goodness of God, church leaders will have to find other motivations to drive them. Frequently, we will turn for help to the sinister twins: duty and debt.

It is not uncommon to hear conference speakers or youth leaders in drill sergeant mode, firing up their listeners with what amounts to little more than a guilt trip. The Christian duty is to "go into all the world," we are told, and only lazy, selfish believers have not already promised the Lord they will go anywhere, anytime if he calls. Since Jesus has done so much for you, how could you refuse him? Christians *can* be cajoled into evangelism like a herd of animals, but this is not a foundation for healthy and effective mission. Duty and debt are cruel motivations for mission. Those who try to draw on them will end up unconvinced salespeople who peddle a product they do not finally believe in or enjoy for themselves.

Deeper still, at the root of these motivations is an undelightful god, who keeps a record of our debts and accepts us in proportion to our performance. Unless Christians are carried into mission by genuine enjoyment of the Lord, their mission will not embody the glory of the living God.

There are also rewards we might set before Christians to engage them in mission. The carrot is mightier than the stick. We might dwell on the capacity of evangelism to deepen our own growth and sanctification. But, in the long run, even "carrots" do not work as ultimate motivations for mission. They are, by nature, *additions* to what believers already have in knowing God and cannot be the primary way the church fuels its mission. Happy mission is rooted not in our response to God but in *his own nature*. The truest and highest motivation for mission is God himself.

## Cutting Out Christ

If we are not captured specifically by the glory of God in Christ, then it will be no surprise when our message quickly has little to do with him. If it is not *him* we are enjoying, it will not be *him* we convey to others. Even unwittingly, we may become ministers of another gospel (Gal. 1:7). It may not be the out-and-out false gospels of, for example, prosperity or "health and wealth," but something more subtle. Our tendency will be toward abstraction from God, focusing on things that, almost without our notice, are not quite Jesus Christ and him crucified. We may find ourselves emphasizing themes of the gospel like "grace" or "heaven" but not explicitly holding out *Christ* as the gift and as the treasure of heaven. We may offer the world the hope of transformed lives, healed hurts, and renewed communities, but make Jesus the *means* to these things rather than the center of them all. These things are blessings of the gospel, but if they are elevated to become its center and our focus, they will become nothing more than substitute gods.

God's mission is revealed in the sending of his Son, and the church is sent with the mission of heralding that same Son. Because of this, the proclamation of the gospel, the heralding of Christ, is the nonnegotiable of mission. Evangelism has *content* to it, and the content is Jesus Christ himself. In other words, our offering to the world is not ourselves but the Lord.

### The God We Know Is the God We Show

If God seems to us to be empty and needy, we will serve him with empty hearts, finally taking what we need from the world rather than freely blessing it. What we truly worship and cherish will, for good or ill, be revealed in our mission. The God we know—or think we know—is the God we will show to the world.

Real, fruitful, healthy mission must begin with delight in God, for we become like the one we worship. His happiness makes us happy; his kindness makes us kind; his glory fills us. Then, made beautiful like our Lord, with compassion and verve we will carry the blessing of Jesus to the ends of the earth.

When Isaiah called the people of Israel to "arise, shine," it was because "your light has come, and *the glory of the* LORD *has risen upon you*" (60:1). This was no frustrated outburst, pushing them to "get up and jolly well get on with it," but a promise that, amid the darkness covering the world, "his glory will be seen upon you" (60:2). The Lord himself was to be with them, enlightening (60:3), enriching (60:5), and beautifying (60:9) them. As God shines upon his beloved redeemed people (60:16), so he will shine *out from* us.

7

# Those Who Look to
# Him Are Radiant

THE FOUNDATION OF ALL OUR MISSION is our knowledge and enjoyment of God.

Yes, I may be born again, but I may not yet be a good missionary. I may have the right intellectual conviction about God's goodness but be unmoved by him. I may know just what to say and how to say it in my gospel presentation, honoring the Lord with my lips while remaining far from him in my heart (Isa. 29:13).

Our delight in God is the main fuel for mission.

## A Good Theologian Is a Good Missionary

John Calvin knew well the vital union between knowing God and mission. Sending missionaries all over the world from

Geneva, he first gave them a solid theological foundation. "He believed that a good missionary had to be a good theologian first."[1] Indeed, a good theologian is a good missionary, *and* a good missionary is a good theologian. Those people who know God most deeply and satisfyingly will be the best at winning hearts into the kingdom; and those most thrilled at the prospect of taking the gospel out into the world are those most captured by the beauty and goodness of the God of the gospel.

This is nothing more than the teaching of Jesus in John 15, who calls his disciples to abide in him, "the true vine," if they would bear fruit (vv. 1–4). The only fruitful branches on the vine are those which abide in him, or specifically abide *in his love* (v. 9). Fruitful mission is certainly an activity: it requires going out and speaking up, and yet it can only be as the *fruit* of branches that have first learned to abide. Our happiness in Jesus's love is his priority for us, even above our sense of being useful to him; in fact, our fruitfulness depends on it.

## The Glorious Ones

The Lord says:

> You are the light of the world. A city set on a hill cannot be hidden. Nor do people light a lamp and put it under a basket, but on a stand, and it gives light to all in the house. In the

same way, *let your light shine before others*, so that they may see your good works and give glory to your Father who is in heaven. (Matt. 5:14–16)

When Christians enjoy union and communion with the Lord, they are transformed into his likeness (2 Cor. 3:18). Where the Lord is present with his people, his very own light and life shine out.

Out of Zion, the perfection of beauty,
*God shines forth.* (Ps. 50:2)

The light and glory of the church are no secondary light and glory but Christ himself.

## When I Am Weak

Mission fueled by the fullness of God is able to deal with the weakness of its missionaries. Wounded soldiers, struggling saints, and stumbling preachers are not dismissed from the Lord's army, because they are not expected to be full in and of themselves. In our suffering, our battle with sin, and our lack of experience or boldness or eloquence, we are nonetheless invited to delight ourselves in the Lord and find fullness in him. Paul's experience with weakness led him to know Christ's power in him so deeply that he was content not to feign personal strength but to renounce it: "For when I am weak, then I am strong" (2 Cor. 12:10).

Even in our sin—our frequent denial of the Lord and of our new life in him—we are not finally empty but know the fullness of God. His mercies never come to an end, and his compassion does not fail (Lam. 3:22). The same Son of God who gave himself for us on the cross is, even now, a sympathetic high priest who continues to intercede for us as we struggle with temptation (Heb. 2:14; 4:15; 7:25).

### Blood and Glory

This matchless love and grace to such empty ones is a fullness that takes us beyond ourselves. Adopted by a perfect Father, united to his glorious Son, and indwelt by the Comforter, Christians are able to take to the spiritual battlefield of mission with happy, humble selflessness.

Suffering in Jesus's service is something we are frequently told to expect. Paul writes, "It has been granted to you that for the sake of Christ you should not only believe in him but also suffer for his sake" (Phil. 1:29), and this is, in fact, a participation in Christ's own sufferings, which are a gateway to resurrection life (Phil. 3:10–11). Peter says that "if you are insulted for the name of Christ, you are *blessed, because the Spirit of glory and of God rests upon you*" (1 Pet. 4:14). On the cross, our captain has gone before us into the fight and has already conquered Satan, sin, and death. He has shed his blood and shown his glory. He has shown us a love that cannot be quenched, even by death (Song 8:6). We cannot lose!

## Outside the Camp

In the law, the camp of Israel and her cities were to be kept ceremonially clean, and all that was defiled had to be ejected. Outside the camp was the only fit place for throwing out ashes and waste (Lev. 4:21); it was the colony of those afflicted with infectious diseases (Lev. 13:46) and the venue for the execution of blasphemers (Lev. 24:14). Yet Jesus went out from the center to prostitutes and tax collectors, lepers and Gentiles. Without being infected or compromised, he embraced them, welcomed them, and saved them. In fact, he himself "suffered outside the [city] gate" on the cross to make his people holy (Heb. 13:12). Because he is so full of purity and holiness, he was not diminished by touching death and disease, but his life blazed out, cleansing and healing, delivering, and making whole. He drove out not just unclean spirits but death itself.

Our own mission now is to "*go to him outside the camp* and bear the reproach he endured" (Heb. 13:13). Made alive, filled, and sanctified in Christ, we do not hide within the "camp" of the church but reach out. This outward stretching of the church, matching that of her Lord, is the extension of his kingdom and blessing into the world, his light shining, and his goodness spreading. Christ's church always moves into the world with a holiness that can bless, purify, and give life.

## A Band of Brothers

Finally, this outward, selfless posture of the church in mission extends to those we find alongside us in the ranks. In a people filled with Jesus's all-embracing glory, there can be no room for tribalism, competition, and hidden agendas.

If I am delightedly filled by Christ, then I will happily march out shoulder to shoulder with brothers and sisters. If I believe that I am brilliant but you are weak, I will trek out alone without any care for you. But if I know my own wretched sinfulness and emptiness, I will be honored to go *together* with you. I will see Christ in you and feel amazed that I can count you a fellow laborer in the gospel (Phil. 2:25). Then, with honesty, humility, trust, and mutual encouragement, we will go out in mission as a happy fellowship.

## Deep Down Delighting

Healthy, robust mission is never an accessory to knowing God. It is not an activist project that must be *added* to our enjoyment of him in salvation. Mission that is to be full and not empty flows only from the satisfaction we experience in Jesus Christ.

The fullness of God given to us in salvation sends us out in mission, but even as we go, we are drawn *toward* fullness too. Our present delight in God magnetically leads us toward the day when we will know his love not in part but in whole. The victories we see in mission as his kingdom advances anticipate the day the whole earth will see his glory.

8

# We Will See Him as He Is

Habakkuk prophesied that

the earth will be filled
 with the knowledge of the glory of the Lord
 as the waters cover the sea. (2:14)

But what will this glory be like? Often when we try to imagine our life in eternity, we soon begin to ponder nervous, slightly guilty questions: Will I recognize my friends and family? Will my dog be there? Will I actually *enjoy* it? Underneath our fears is the suspicion that when God finally and fully reveals his glory—the weight and substance of his being and nature—it will turn out to be something *other* than the grace, goodness, and kindness displayed in the gospel. The self-giving glory of the cross will have been simply a means to another end: perhaps God's retirement to a life of isolated majesty, with troublesome humanity out of his hair.

Wonderfully, we could not be more wrong about God's plans.

## The Revelation of Jesus Christ

The last book of the Bible is specifically about "the revelation of Jesus Christ" (Rev. 1:1) because it is *his* glory that will be fully unveiled on the last day. All the promises of God—including those about our future—find their "Yes" *in Jesus* (2 Cor. 1:20). In the gospel's promised future, we will eternally enjoy the very glory that fuels our lives and mission today. When Jesus returns, the spark of our *present* enjoyment of God and his gospel will be fanned into flame as all creation is saturated with the glory of our own dear Lord Jesus, the radiance of the Father.

The glory that we long for and hold out to the world is the very same outshining glory that propels our mission now.

## God's Last Great End

This glorious end to the story is both the goal and the motivation of mission because it has *always* been God's design and intention for his creation. From the very beginning to the very end, God's purpose in all things is the demonstration of his glory. But the God who has been so selflessly kind to us throughout history is not planning to exit stage left with a selfish flourish of megalomania.

No, God has determined that his own outshining brings about *our* delight and joy in the end. He is *already* eternally happy in fellowship with his Son, and *that* is what will overflow to us and all creation in the end. God will make us eternally happy out of the sheer abundance of his own happiness.

## Gracious Glory

Jesus's description of our "eternal life" in John 17:3 is specifically about enjoying fellowship with God: "that they know you, the only true God, and Jesus Christ whom you have sent." The life and glory that will one day fill the earth springs from the fountain of the everlasting love and delight of the Father, Son, and Spirit.

In this glory, we who are naturally far from God and tragically self-absorbed will be made eternally joyful and content, enfolded into indestructible fellowship with God. We who are in Christ will be drawn in to know and enjoy him further and more deeply than ever before, knowing in full what we now know only in part, seeing with crisp clarity what we now see only dimly of his beauty (1 Cor. 13:12). For God himself will come to *dwell with us* (Rev. 21:3). The one who once came as a "friend of tax collectors and sinners" (Luke 7:34) and loved them to death will prove himself devoted to us for endless ages.

On the last day, just as at Calvary, God who is full of life, light, and love will *pour himself out* for those who are naturally empty, gloomy, and unlovely. Flowing to us from the cross, his is an entirely *gracious* glory.

## All Things New

The personal presence of the Lord will mean that all that has saddened and hurt us will be blasted away. The Lamb on heaven's throne will declare, "Behold, I am making all things new" (Rev. 21:5). God himself "will wipe away every tear from their eyes, and death shall be no more, neither shall there be mourning, nor crying, nor pain anymore, for the former things have passed away" (Rev. 21:4). He will finally drive out Satan and all evil from the world (Rev. 20:10). Death, the final enemy, will be destroyed, and all will be perfect, everlasting life (1 Cor. 15:26). You will have cried your last tear, grappled with guilt's last assault, suffered your last bereavement. For when the glory of the Lord fills the earth, we will live in a world with no more threat of danger, disease, and death.

What a hope to share with the world! In the drying of our tears, we see a God so filled with compassion that he personally stoops to comfort his people. In the last defeat of Satan, we see a God so beautifully pure that he will tolerate nothing that would harm his children. In the end of death, we see a God so generously full that he loves to give his life without measure such that death is blotted out forever. The hope of his coming is comfort for the weeping, the oppressed, and the dying today. *As we hold out the hope of the gospel in our broken world now, it is the full revelation of the loving God of the gospel that we anticipate.*

## A World of Love

The defining characteristic of our future fellowship with God is his love for us. For God *is* love (1 John 4:8) and "love never ends" (1 Cor. 13:8).

In the life to come, we will love God more truly because we will finally have an unclouded appreciation of his love for us. Our love for others will also be transformed. In the light of God's love in heaven, nothing and nobody will be unlovely.

Can you imagine a life where you *know*, without any creeping anxiety, that you are perfectly and totally loved by God? Where you love him in return without any whisper of shame or inadequacy? A life where you are entirely secure in the love of those around you and are able to love them all without feeling exposed or vulnerable? Where you love people with such a generous freedom that you yourself only become more open and lovely?

This is life in the glory of God and the light of the Lamb who was slain. The grace we have found at the foot of the cross we will discover again and again in wave after infinite wave: the free giving of the superabundant one to those who are in themselves empty, needy, and longing.

## Children of the Light

The promise of this life before us sustains us now in our ministry and mission. And it is precisely this hope that we hold out to the world.

Our mission carries the same glory as our hope. In 1 Thessalonians 5, Paul calls Christians "children of light," who do not belong to the darkness of this present and passing age (vv. 4–6). Because believers are filled with the life of Christ by the Spirit, we are lights in "this present darkness" (Eph. 6:12), beacons of divine glory in a sea of emptiness. In a sense, Christians are children of the future, living in the world with their sights set beyond it, knowing what is coming soon.

The church's mission is shaped and driven by the very nature of our God. All that we know of him, however limited by our present ignorance and sin, fills us with joy. Yet our hope of knowing him fully in the age to come can only increase our delight and anticipation, propelling us out into the world in overwhelmed gladness.

## Happily Ever After

There is a reason that all the best stories end with a bride and groom living happily ever after: it is the one true story in the universe. At the end, Jesus Christ will fulfill his vows to his church.

The final mention of the Lamb in the book of Revelation comes in chapter 21 when he is married to his blood-bought bride. She is "the holy city Jerusalem coming down out of heaven from God, *having the glory of God*, its radiance like a most rare jewel" (vv. 10–11). This had been his heart's desire from the beginning (Song 2:10; Hos. 2:20). Yes, the culmination of history is the glory of God. Not glory taken but glory *given*. The whole creation suffused with his light, his creatures filled and made happy in his goodness, his bride drenched eternally in his love. We, the redeemed, can only sing,

> Worthy is the Lamb who was slain,
> to receive power and wealth and wisdom and might
> and honor and glory and blessing! (Rev. 5:12)

# Notes

*Chapter 5: Born in Zion*

1. Henry Van Dyke, "Joyful, Joyful, We Adore Thee" (1907), https://hymnary.org.

*Chapter 7: Those Who Look to Him Are Radiant*

1. Frank A. James III, "Calvin the Evangelist," *Reformed Quarterly* 19, no. 2 (2001): 8.

# Scripture Index

# Union

**We fuel reformation in churches and lives.**

Union Publishing invests in the next generation of leaders with theology that gives them a taste for a deeper knowledge of God. From books to our free online content, we are committed to producing excellent resources that will refresh, transform, and grow believers and their churches.

We want people everywhere to know, love, and enjoy God, glorifying him in everything they do. For this reason, we've collected hundreds of free articles, podcasts, book chapters, and video content for our free online collection. We also produce a fresh stream of written, audio, and video resources to help you to be more fully alive in the truth, goodness, and beauty of Jesus.

If you are hungry for reformational resources that will help you delight in God and grow in Christ, we'd love for you to visit us at unionpublishing.org.

**unionpublishing.org**

# Union Series

  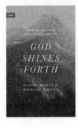 

**Full & Concise Editions**

*Rejoice and Tremble* | *What Does It Mean to Fear the Lord?*

*Deeper* | *How Does God Change Us?*

*The Loveliest Place* | *Why Should We Love the Local Church?*

*God Shines Forth* | *What Fuels the Mission of the Church?*

The Union series invites readers to experience deeper enjoyment
of God through four interconnected values: delighting in God,
growing in Christ, serving the church, and blessing the world.

For more information, visit **crossway.org**.

"Dustin Benge provides us with an absolute gem—a beautiful condensation of all that is good about the local church. With ease of prose, Benge introduces us to the multicolored facets of what the church is and how she functions to grow us into the people of God. A marvelous read."

**Derek W. H. Thomas,** Senior Minister, First Presbyterian Church, Columbia, South Carolina; Teaching Fellow, Ligonier Ministries; Chancellor's Professor, Reformed Theological Seminary

"The true and faithful church is the beautiful bride of Christ. In the experience of reading this refreshing treatment, all who love the church will rejoice in the realization of her beauty. Many people are concerned about how the world views the church. The world will never have the right perspective until the church itself sees her beauty. Surely this is what the apostle Paul meant when he said in 2 Corinthians 11:2 that he desired to present the church as a chaste virgin to Christ. This book is a much-needed gift to the people of God."

**John MacArthur,** Pastor, Grace Community Church, Sun Valley, California; Chancellor, The Master's University and Seminary

"This is a rich reflection upon the nature of the church. Benge rightly shows us the way the church is viewed from heaven and from the eschaton. If we could only grasp the glorious beauty of the church in the light of these two perspectives, the negativity that too often crosses our lips and permeates our minds about the triune God's beloved would be replaced with wonder and awe. Warmly recommended."

**Michael A. G. Haykin,** Chair and Professor of Church History, The Southern Baptist Theological Seminary

"A little more than a decade ago I said I'd never seen such a profound unity in the church. What has happened? Leadership failures, unresolved conflicts, high-profile apostasies, political division, social upheaval, a global pandemic, theological controversy, and more. Is greater church unity possible again? Of course it is, but any movement toward unity must be dependent on the Holy Spirit and based on God's truth. May the Lord use this book, in which Dustin Benge faithfully sets forth the glories of God's truth about the church, to rebuild our unity."

**Donald S. Whitney,** Professor of Biblical Spirituality and Associate Dean, The Southern Baptist Theological Seminary

"Do you consider the church to be lovely? Jesus does. He looks at his blood-bought bride with deep delight and desires that we do the same. In *Why Should We Love the Local Church?* Dustin Benge introduces us afresh to the church in a way that rekindles affection and renews commitment. Many books tell us about the church, but few help us love the church. This important work refreshes the soul and inspires worship."

**Garrett Kell,** Lead Pastor, Del Ray Baptist Church, Alexandria, Virginia

"Beholding the true beauty of the church can often be a challenge because many times she is torn asunder by various scandals and divisions. Dustin Benge nevertheless calls us to view the church from the divine perspective as the chosen bride of Christ. Only through this corrective lens can we recognize how precious she is in the sight of our triune God. May God give us eyes to see her radiant glory as she is clothed with the glistening garments of Christ."

**Steven J. Lawson,** President, OnePassion Ministries; Professor of Preaching, The Master's Seminary; Teaching Fellow, Ligonier Ministries

*WHY SHOULD WE LOVE*
*THE LOCAL CHURCH?*

**Union**

A book series edited by Michael Reeves

*Rejoice and Tremble: The Surprising Good News of the Fear of the Lord*, Michael Reeves (2021)

*What Does It Mean to Fear the Lord?*, Michael Reeves (2021, concise version of *Rejoice and Tremble*)

*Deeper: Real Change for Real Sinners*, Dane C. Ortlund (2021)

*How Does God Change Us?*, Dane C. Ortlund (2021, concise version of *Deeper*)

*The Loveliest Place: The Beauty and Glory of the Church*, Dustin Benge (2022)

*Why Should We Love the Local Church?*, Dustin Benge (2022, concise version of *The Loveliest Place*)

# WHY SHOULD WE LOVE THE LOCAL CHURCH?

*DUSTIN BENGE*

WHEATON, ILLINOIS

**Library of Congress Cataloging-in-Publication Data**

Names: Benge, Dustin W., author.
Title: Why should we love the local church? / Dustin Benge.
Other titles: Loveliest place
Description: Wheaton, Illinois : Crossway, 2022. | Series: Union | Includes bibliographical references and index.
Identifiers: LCCN 2021023824 (print) | LCCN 2021023825 (ebook) | ISBN 9781433574986 (trade paperback) | ISBN 9781433574993 (pdf) | ISBN 9781433575006 (mobipocket) | ISBN 9781433575013 (epub)
Subjects: LCSH: Church.
Classification: LCC BV600.3 .B46252 2022 (print) | LCC BV600.3 (ebook) | DDC 262.001/7—dc23
LC record available at https://lccn.loc.gov/2021023824
LC ebook record available at https://lccn.loc.gov/2021023825

Crossway is a publishing ministry of Good News Publishers.

| VP | | | 31 | 30 | 29 | 28 | 27 | 26 | 25 | 24 | 23 | 22 |
|----|----|----|----|----|----|----|----|----|----|----|----|----|
| 15 | 14 | 13 | 12 | 11 | 10 | 9 | 8 | 7 | 6 | 5 | 4 | 3 | 2 | 1 |

*To Nate Pickowicz,*
*my friend, brother,*
*and co-laborer in the gospel*

# Contents

# Series Preface

OUR INNER CONVICTIONS and values shape our lives and our ministries. And at Union—the cooperative ministries of Union School of Theology, Union Publishing, Union Research, and Union Mission (visit www.theolo.gy)—we long to grow and support men and women who will delight in God, grow in Christ, serve the church, and bless the world. This Union series of books is an attempt to express and share those values.

They are values that flow from the beauty and grace of God. The living God is so glorious and kind, he cannot be known without being adored. Those who truly know him will love him, and without that heartfelt delight in God, we are nothing but hollow hypocrites. That adoration of God necessarily works itself out in a desire to grow in Christlikeness. It also fuels a love for Christ's precious bride, the church, and a desire

humbly to serve—rather than use—her. And, lastly, loving God brings us to share his concerns, especially to see his life-giving glory fill the earth.

Each exploration of a subject in the Union series will appear in two versions: a full volume and a concise one. The concise treatments, such as this one, are like shorter guided tours: they stick to the main streets and move on fast. You may find, at the end of this little book, that you have questions or want to explore some more: in that case, the fuller volume will take you further up and further in.

My hope and prayer is that these books will bless you and your church as you develop a deeper delight in God that overflows in joyful integrity, humility, Christlikeness, love for the church, and a passion to make disciples of all nations.

*Michael Reeves*
SERIES EDITOR

# Introduction

WE ALL HAVE SPECIAL PLACES we visit, either in person or in memory. For me, one of those treasured places is the farm of my grandparents. Running through freshly plowed fields, climbing majestic oaks, and sitting at the table of my grandmother's cooking—there's no place I would rather be. This place evokes a sense of joy, comfort, and home.

When we think of the church, does it arouse similar deep affection? Can we say the church is one of those unique places that conjures a sincere sense of longing, delight, and home?

It's all too easy to allow our warmth toward the church to slip away, as we grow cold and apathetic. Honestly, the church can often be a difficult place to think of as *lovely*. However, when we shift our perspective from our puny self-interest, which often fuels our disgruntlement toward the church, she not only becomes precious to us but also becomes a treasure of eternal joy, beauty, and glory.

This book is about the loveliness, beauty, and glory of the church. It's for all those who sometimes struggle to see those qualities in her. If you tirelessly serve within her ministries while dismayed by her apparent failures, or have rare, unsustainable glimpses of her beauty, this book is for you. The singular goal is to awaken your affections. Not affections for form, methodology, structure, organization, or programs, but affections for *who* she is and *why* she exists.

There is no more robust and doxological foundation upon which we can build a definition of the church than the eternal work of the Father, Son, and Holy Spirit. In the words of eighteenth-century New England pastor-theologian Jonathan Edwards, the whole world was created so that "the eternal Son of God might obtain a spouse."[1] The church is not a Trinitarian afterthought in response to man's fall in the garden—quite the contrary. The church is the focused domain where all God's presence, promises, and purposes are unveiled and eternally realized.

The church's beauty and loveliness are most vividly portrayed in the brilliant metaphor of her as the "bride of Christ." In his instructions to husbands regarding the love they should have for their wives, the apostle Paul writes, "Love your wives, as Christ loved the church and gave himself up for her" (Eph. 5:25). This stunning bride is arrayed in snow-white garments washed in the redeeming blood of Christ (Rev. 7:14), and beholding her beauty, a vast multitude cries out,

> The marriage of the Lamb has come,
>     and his Bride has made herself ready. (Rev. 19:7)

God gives the church to Christ as his bride, Edwards says, "so that the mutual joys between this bride and bridegroom are the end of the creation."[2]

As the creation of God, the church is a means through which the Father delights in Christ as the object of his eternal love and divine happiness. The church's life is beautifully framed by her position as the reward to Christ for his suffering on the cross, thus making Christ a worthy groom for his bride. This glorious union between Christ and his church will never be severed. The two, joined together by God, are eternally satisfied in one another as they bask in the glory, majesty, and holiness of God.

This book has one aim: to set before you a thoroughly biblical portrait of the church that derives its life from the sweet fellowship of the Father, Son, and Spirit, creating a community of love, worship, fellowship, and mission, all animated by the gospel and empowered by the word of God.

By beholding such radiant beauty and loveliness, may we lift our collective and worshipful cry, "Indeed, the church is the loveliest place on earth."

# You Are Beautiful

*Behold, you are beautiful, my love;*
*behold, you are beautiful.*
SONG OF SOLOMON 1:15

THE CHURCH HAS PLAYED a central role in many of our lives. She has nurtured in times of grief, shepherded in valleys of despair, and instructed in seasons of growth.

We love her people. We love her ministries. We love her worship. We love her teaching. We love her comfort.

Do we love her?

### Admired by Christ

Reflecting on Song of Solomon 1:15, John Gill, an eighteenth-century English Baptist pastor, wrote, "These are the words of

Christ, commending the beauty of the church, expressing his great affection for her, and his high esteem of her; of her fairness and beauty."[1] Gill interprets Song of Solomon as an intense allegorical portrayal of the love, union, and communion that exists between Jesus Christ and his bride, the church. The bridegroom fixes his eternal attention upon the bride and identifies her as "beautiful."

What must it be like to be admired by the sinless Son of God? Rather than admire her, we imagine he would identify her failures, her shortcomings, and the loathsome sin that so often spoils her garments.

The church is beautiful because the lens through which Christ regards her is his cross—the focal point of blood, righteousness, forgiveness, union, justification, regeneration, and grace. Ultimately, the cross of the Lord Jesus Christ makes her beautiful. It is his sacrificial, substitutionary, sinless blood that washes her garments as white as snow. The cross of Christ makes her beautiful not only inwardly by justification but also outwardly through sanctification. From giving second birth to final glory, the righteousness of Christ creates a beautiful bride.

### Reflected Beauty

The supreme expression of God's beauty is his Son, Jesus Christ, who himself is the image and radiance of his Father. Paul affirms Jesus as "the image of God" (2 Cor. 4:4). That is, to see Jesus is to see God, to hear Jesus is to hear God, to know Jesus is to know God. In Colossians 1:15, Paul classifies Jesus as "the image of the invisible God." As glory is a defining characteristic of God's nature, the beauty that shines forth from God also shines forth from Jesus, for Jesus is the visible incarnation of God's radiant glory.

To express God's infinite love for Christ, God gives him a spouse, the church. The church is a gift from God to his Son "so that," according to Jonathan Edwards, "the mutual joys between this bride and bridegroom are the end of creation."[2] Therefore, as the Son is a reflection of his Father, the church, as his eternal bride, is a reflection of the Son.

When Christ lovingly looks upon his bride and exclaims that she is "beautiful," he beholds the reflection of the everlasting glory and infinite love of his Father, who is the primary fountain from which all true beauty flows.

The church is beautiful because God is beautiful.

## The Bride's Affection

Not only does Christ lavish his affection upon the church as the object of his joyful love, but the church also reveres her bridegroom with the same unshakable devotion. She describes him as "distinguished among ten thousand" (Song 5:10), having "lips

. . . dripping liquid myrrh" (v. 13), "arms . . . set with jewels" (v. 14), "legs . . . set on bases of gold" (v. 15), and "altogether desirable" (v. 16).

Of all who might arrest her attention, Jesus Christ is better than all the rest because he has purchased the church with his blood (Acts 20:28). Christ is beautiful to the church because he rescued her from her enemies and set her in heavenly places (Eph. 2:6). Christ is beautiful to the church because he freely offered his life as payment for a debt she owed (John 10:11). Christ is beautiful to the church because he satisfied God's wrath against her sin and victoriously conquered death (Rom. 3:24–25). Christ is her Savior. Christ is her Redeemer. Christ is her beauty.

## 2

# The Household of God

*I will be glory in her midst.*

ZECHARIAH 2:5

GOD RESIDES EXPLICITLY in a distinctive and familial way among his people. God dwells in heaven in the sense that his glory, majesty, and holiness are on display there in particular richness. Yet he also assures his people that he will "be glory in [their] midst" (Zech. 2:5).

Moved by his inexhaustible love for the church before the foundation of the world, God resides in her midst with "every spiritual blessing in the heavenly places" (Eph. 1:3), so that even now those who are part of his family on earth are "seated . . . with him in the heavenly places in Christ Jesus" (Eph. 2:6).

21

## God's Family

Defining the church in institutional terms is futile, for the church belongs exclusively to God. In 1 Timothy 3:15, Paul offers instructions in godliness so that we may know how "to behave in the *household of God*, which is the church of the living God." The word "household" elicits a metaphor not of a building or structure but of a family—those within the same house.

We are brothers and sisters to Christ through our second birth into his family (John 1:12–13). By nature, we are born in sin, wholly separated from God, but in Christ, we are adopted into God's family. Reading the New Testament is like looking through a family picture album or hearing the family history recited by a grandparent. The church is God's household and our family.

## Defining Home

The church is defined by many words and phrases that identify her as being of heavenly origin. The English word *church* originates from the Greek term for those who belong to the Lord. This word derives from a title given to God as the sovereign Master over a people. The church is, therefore, God's special possession over which he resides as Master.

The church is most regularly associated with the Greek word *ekklēsia*, a term meaning "those who are called out" or "an assembly of the people." The church is uniquely those who have been called out of sinful darkness by God the Father through salvation in Jesus Christ, are now sealed by the Holy Spirit, and now belong to the Lord. The church thus finds her origin, beauty, and perfection in the triune God.

## The Assembly of Mount Zion

Throughout his voluminous works, John Owen, a seventeenth-century Puritan theologian, offers a vivid image and description of the church. In his 1645 *Greater Catechism* he writes, "The whole company of God's elect, called of God, by the Word and Spirit, out of their natural condition, to the dignity of his children, and united unto Christ their head, by faith, in the bond of the Spirit."[1] Consistent with Paul's detailed description of those who are the church in Ephesians 1, Owen is careful to characterize the church as a Trinitarian and heavenly family made up of those whom God elects, calls, and unites to Christ through his lavish grace.

By definition, the church is constituted in a particular form. Various characteristics mark her: celebration of worship, preaching of the gospel, making disciples, the exercise of discipline, mutual edification, and the work of evangelism.[2] The church is best defined by both universal and local terminology. Theologians sometimes refer to these two categories as "invisible" and "visible." The invisible church is composed of believers worldwide, who have been elected, called, and regenerated. The visible church is those redeemed believers within a local congregation.

## God's Home, Forever

Our one hope is the constant abiding presence of God—forever—which assures the church that God has not forsaken, nor will he ever forsake, his home. He will never love the church any less than he always has. He will never divorce the church. He will never go searching for a more attractive family. He will never move out or move away. The cascade of his love to her will never dissolve, for it runs from eternity past to eternity future.

God doesn't begrudgingly give himself to the church. He doesn't bemoan the home he has made among us. He doesn't regret pursuing us with his everlasting love. God delights to make the church his household and makes her beautiful by his presence among her.

3

# Our Father and Friend

*O Lord, you are our Father;*
*we are the clay, and you are the potter;*
*we are all the work of your hand.*

ISAIAH 64:8

TO DEFINE THE CHURCH as a mere earthly institution or some entrepreneur's vision would be to miss completely who the church is in God's eternal mind and heart. The church's beauty comes into indefectible focus only when we peer through the lens of God's relationship to her. Anything less is choosing to play in mud puddles while refusing the vastness of the ocean.

## Our Father

In Matthew 6, the disciples request that Jesus teach them how to pray. Jesus offers them something entirely unexpected to their old covenant way of thinking. He constructs a short prayer that serves as a pattern for all our conversations with God. While the prayer contains all the elements one might expect, Jesus addresses God using a personal name somewhat foreign to the Old Testament theological mind.

Under the old covenant, the children of God approached him in fear and trembling through the ritualism of priesthood and sacrifice. To enter his holy presence, the Israelites were required to meet with God through the tablernacle and temple. Though God was as much of a Father to believers in the Old Testament as he is in the New, Jesus brings God eternally close to the heart of the believer and invites us to bypass the priests, animal sacrifices, veils, and temples by offering us a vividly affectionate relationship with the sovereign of the universe: "Our Father in heaven" (Matt. 6:9).

God is the Father to his children in a way he is not to anyone else. He isn't only *a* Father or *the* Father, but he is *our* Father. He uniquely loves his church. The love of the Father always precedes our love toward him (1 John 4:19).

What does it mean for the church to call God "our Father"?

First, it's the end of self-exaltation. To confess that God is our Father is to acknowledge that we are helpless creatures and cannot rescue ourselves, for we need a Father who watches over us to save, protect, guide, and help. Second, calling God "our Father" means that specific fears should cease. To enter into a loving relationship with a loving Father through a loving Son eliminates any fear we could ever have of the wrath of God against our sin. Third, it brings an end to our hopelessness. There's no greater hope that children can have in a life wrecked by sin, shame, and despair than to be in the arms of a devoted, loving heavenly Father. It's also an end of loneliness. As our Father, God grants the church an intimacy and relationship with him that is all her own.

Is there anyone who knows all our failures and still loves us? Is there anyone who can give meaning to our hopeless lives? Is there anyone who can wipe away rolling tears? Our Father can.

## Our Friend

Genuine friendship is more than action; it's devotion. When this devotion is the lens through which the church views God's company with us, that reality is so inexhaustible that it defies comprehension. God's benevolent offering of his beloved Son is most brightly on display in the Son's willingness to offer his life a ransom for his Father's friends: "Greater love has no one than this, that someone lay down his life for his friends" (John 15:13). And since the Father freely gave us his beloved Son, "how will he not also with him graciously give us all things?" (Rom. 8:32).

God holds his friends beautifully close to his heart from everlasting to everlasting. He doesn't abandon his church for a better, more faithful, or more loyal friend. He's never lamented choosing the church as his friend. When God established his friendship with the church, it had absolutely nothing to do with our faithfulness to him and everything to do with his faithfulness to us.

Through the millennia of the church's existence, her history often paints a disturbing picture of unfaithfulness, coldness, error, lethargy, and the like. But her friendship with God gives the church great comfort that though she may wander off the path at certain junctures, he always remains her faithful friend (Jer. 31:31–33; Heb. 8:8–10). There has never been a time in her patchy history, nor will there be a time in her future, when God will deny his friend, forsake his friend, or cast his friend aside.

God is both a Father and a friend to the church. These cherished relationships remind the church that God isn't remote and distant but is near and close. We are eternally bound to our Father and friend. He is uniquely ours, and we are uniquely his.

# Our Savior and Head

*Christ is the head of the church,*
*his body, and is himself its Savior.*

EPHESIANS 5:23

TO GRASP CHRIST'S LOVE for his church is to plumb depths that have no bottom, find a treasure with no bounds, and climb heights that have no peak. All our redemption and salvation flows freely from that never-ending fountain of divine love. And such boundless love can only rightly be understood by visiting a bloody cross and an empty tomb.

## Our Savior

The Greek word translated "Savior" means "one who preserves or rescues from natural dangers and afflictions." It carries the idea of deliverance from harm in order to preserve. A Savior is both a rescuer and protector. In his prophecy of the Messiah, Zechariah affirms that this anointed one will deliver us from the "hand of our enemies" (Luke 1:74). Who are our enemies, and why do we need rescuing? We need rescuing from our sin, God's wrath upon our sin, and death, which is a consequence of our sin (Isa. 59:2).

Jesus doesn't just excuse our sin and tell us to ignore its consequences. Christ and his bride are so intimately identified that they become united with one another in death and resurrection. Sinners come to the cross of Christ and receive, by faith, the wages of their sin—death. We don't die physically, but we die a required death through Christ, for he becomes our substitute and stands in our stead, taking upon himself the unmitigated wrath of his Father. What God requires of us because of our sin is paid in full by our beloved, the Lord Jesus Christ.

This beautiful union is so fixed and permanent that we are now taken into the eternal love that exists between the Father and the Son through the Spirit. The same love that flows unceasingly between the Father and the Son now directly flows to the bride.

Jesus is a worthy Savior not only because of his union with the nature and love of his Father but also because of union with the nature and love of his bride. He unites to her as she places her faith in him and thus he becomes the ground of her rescue and redemption. The bridegroom takes death upon himself and offers his meritorious work freely to his bride, that she may be welcomed into his family.

## Our Head

The relationship between Christ and his bride is so multifaceted that merely one title will not satisfy all its beauty. Numerous rich metaphors throughout Scripture depict this divine exchange:

- Christ is both her founder and her foundation.
- Christ is both her Judge and her Savior.
- Christ is both her lover and her beloved.
- Christ is both her preserver and her hope.
- Christ is both her righteousness and her holiness.

However, perhaps no metaphorical phrase comes close to the gravity of Christ being the *head* of the church. Uniting himself to us in our nature not only makes Jesus a fit Savior for his bride but also makes him a fit head.

The phrase "head of the church" is not employed to identify Christ as the head of a company or the head of an organization. In Ephesians 5:23, Paul distinguishes Christ as "the head of the church, *his body.*" The church isn't the result of human ingenuity. The living Christ is the head of a living organism.

Identifying Christ as the church's head denotes that he has sovereign lordship and supreme authority over her. As Jesus told his disciples when he commissioned them to evangelize the nations, "All authority in heaven and on earth has been given to me" (Matt. 28:18). The church doesn't belong to pastors or church members; the church belongs to Christ, and he is its sovereign head.

The church is intimately united to Christ as her Savior and head. This glorious truth will be the theme of the new song the bride will trumpet forth throughout the heavens:

> Worthy are you to take the scroll
>     and to open its seals,
> for you were slain, and by your blood you ransomed
>         people for God
>     from every tribe and language and people and nation.
>         (Rev. 5:9)

# Our Helper and Beautifier

*I will ask the Father, and he will*
*give you another Helper.*

ANY DISCUSSION ON THE CHURCH would be severely lacking without a close look at the presence and ministry of the Holy Spirit. Without him, the church would never have been founded. Godly leaders would never have been called, believers added, gifts distributed, service rendered, or growth realized.

## Our Helper

To comfort the hearts of his despondent disciples, who have just learned that Jesus will soon be leaving them, he promises them a "Helper" (John 14:16). The word used in reference to the Holy Spirit means "one called to another's side, specifically to help and aid." It can also refer to an intercessor, an assistant, or one who pleads another's cause before a judge. The word itself reveals the all-encompassing role of the Spirit within the body of Christ. He is our Helper, Intercessor, Assistant, Advocate, Comforter, Counselor, and Sustainer.

What love Jesus has for the church! He doesn't leave her to fend for herself with her own devices, inventions, creativity, or wit. The Holy Spirit is sufficient to equip and empower you to discharge every aspect of the turning-the-world-upside-down ministry to which Jesus has called his church.

## Our Beautifier

A chief work of the Spirit is to bring beauty out of chaos. In creation, the Spirit brought harmony out of formlessness and void (Gen. 1:2). In redemption, the Spirit brings life out of death and sin (John 3:5–6, 8). In sanctification, the Spirit brings beauty out of fallen flesh and wayward hearts (Rom. 8:9–11). The church becomes an instrument of Christ's beaming radiance in the world through the individual expressions of the work of grace by the Spirit in the lives of believers.

There's perhaps no better or more familiar expression of the Holy Spirit's beautifying work within the church than

Galatians 5:22–23, "The fruit of the Spirit is love, joy, peace, patience, kindness, goodness, faithfulness, gentleness, self-control."

At our salvation, the Spirit could instantaneously make us holy in action, word, and deed. However, he chooses instead to produce fruit in our lives to authenticate our union with Christ. Bearing fruit is a sign that we are *in* Christ, and he is *in* us.

*Love.* This is not the butterflies-in-the-stomach first-date kind of love or the tear-welling love at the reunion of friends. This is the sacrificial love that is conscious not of self-fulfillment but of self-giving. This kind of love is absolute in its resolve regardless of the response in return.

*Joy.* When the buds of joy blossom on the branch, the Spirit is generating more than mere happiness. The result is a joy unconditionally independent of the circumstances around us. The Spirit beautifies the church by anchoring her hope not in a kind of slap-happy giddiness so characteristic of worldly happiness, but in a joy founded on God himself.

*Peace.* This form of tranquil peace pillows our head amid the storms of life in the conscious assurance that our sovereign God is the controller of every infinitesimal detail and is working all things for our good and his ultimate glory (Rom. 8:28).

*Patience.* The Spirit beautifies the bride of Christ by producing within her self-restraint that doesn't retaliate. It never seeks revenge for wrongs done. It faces ever-arduous situations. It always endures.

*Kindness.* The Spirit desires to beautify the church by creating succulent fruit on the branch that yields the sweetness of our tender care for fellow believers and unbelievers alike, those inside the church and those outside

*Goodness.* This fruit conveys a determined resolve always to serve in the presence of God. In rejoicing, rebuke, exhortation, even in times of discipline, goodness toward wayward brothers and sisters keeps us beautifully demonstrating to every spectator that there are no perfect people—there is only a perfect Savior.

*Faithfulness.* Faithfulness is a work of the Holy Spirit (Acts 6:5). He beautifies the church through the fruit of faithfulness exhibited in her commitment and loyalty in serving others through Christ.

*Gentleness.* This fruit has been called "meekness" and speaks of a gentle blowing breeze that hints at strength but holds back in power. This isn't cowardice but is debased humility that keeps its power in check. Through the Spirit, the church can turn the world upside down through controlled humility.

*Self-control.* How utterly miserable we are at keeping our actions, minds, and hearts in check. How vitally necessary it is that the Holy Spirit grow this fruit upon the branches of our hearts. To be self-controlled is a command—a command to submit to the will of God at all times, in all circumstances, abandoning our selfish desires and sinful pleasures.

Christ sent the Holy Spirit to be both Helper and beautifier of the church. Fully deserving of our worship, the Spirit accomplishes a work in each believer, and thereby in the body of Christ, that should be recognized as tantamount to the works of both the Father and the Son.

# A Pillar and Buttress of Truth

*. . . a pillar and buttress of the truth.*

1 TIMOTHY 3:15

WHAT CAN WE DO when the lies of this present age spring a leak in the church, which is supposed to hold back the torrent of the world's scheming deception? Some within the church would like to run for higher ground, cloistering themselves away from this growing danger. Others consider themselves impervious to the peril and rush to swim in the streams of the world, thinking they will never be polluted, only to end up drowning in the rushing waters of compromise. Still others, quite sincerely, just don't know how to respond.

## Twisted Truth

Throughout the millennia since his fall, Satan has not altered his strategy of deceit. He has inundated every societal level with confusion and falsehood, from government, educational systems, mass media, and the family, to even the church. Paul warned the church at Corinth, "I am afraid that as the serpent deceived Eve by his cunning, your thoughts will be led astray from a sincere and pure devotion to Christ" (2 Cor. 11:3). Satan delights in leading the church away from faithful obedience to God and his word by inviting her members to swim and frolic in the waters of worldly lies. Unless we are held captive by God's word, the very heart of the church is susceptible to Satan's cunning deception. This is why, surrounded by a world of lies, the church must be ready to answer with God's truth.

## Bearing Witness

Paul describes the church as the "pillar and buttress of the truth" (1 Tim. 3:15). That's a vivid way of saying that it's the church's task to *uphold* the truth. The Greek word for "buttress" means "support." This is the only time this word appears in the New Testament, and it defines the church as a bulwark of God's truth. The truth is her mission. The truth is her message. The truth is her reason for existing in the world.

In Paul's meticulous description, he is saying that once God's truth is removed from the church, her humanly devised structures, programs, and purpose for existing will collapse.

During the final moments of his life, standing before Pontius Pilate, Jesus declared that the reason he came into the world was to "bear witness to the truth." He added, "Everyone who is of the truth listens to my voice" (John 18:37). Notice in his stunning testimony that Jesus proclaimed that he came to bear witness to *the* truth—not a vague, obscure, nebulous, open-to-one's-own-interpretation kind of truth. Jesus came to bear witness to only one truth, God's truth, the only truth that exists. The only truth that will still be standing when heaven and earth pass away (Matt. 24:35).

Jesus is the full and definitive expression of God's absolute truth (Heb. 1:1–4). His whole ministry fulfilled the divine charge of truth-bearer. It was prophesied that Jesus would be "full of . . . truth" (John 1:14). He called himself "the truth" (John 14:6). The entirety of Jesus's teaching and preaching ministry was characterized as "the way of God truthfully" (Matt. 22:16).

## All Scripture

The truth meant to be heralded by the church is found in a book. Paul identifies that book in 2 Timothy 3:16: "All Scripture is breathed out by God and profitable for teaching, for reproof, for correction, and for training in righteousness."

Paul doesn't say that the Bible is "breathed upon by God"; Scripture is "breathed out by God." God's word is God's breath. And this divine breath brings life to his church, molding and shaping us into the image of Christ, sanctifying and renewing our hearts, maturing our churches, and making them a gloriously beautiful place.

The truth given to us through Scripture is the pillar and buttress of the church, having the same authority, relevance, and sufficiency as God himself, for the Bible is his divine breath.

How does the church proclaim the truth of Christ in an ever-deeper cesspool of lies? First, she must separate herself and boldly refuse to be conformed to this present world—she must be continually transformed into imitators of Christ (Rom. 12:2; 1 Cor. 11:1). Second, the church must proclaim the countercultural truth of God's word, in love, before a hostile and unbelieving world (Col. 4:2–6). We must lovingly herald every command, commendation, and condemnation of Scripture. Third, the church must develop discerning wisdom, bringing every outside word captive to the obedience of Christ (2 Cor. 10:5). The world, full of hate, lies, deception, murder, half-truth, and even death, is illuminated by this light. So be what you are—pillars and buttresses of the truth in a world of lies.

# In Spirit and Truth

*True worshipers will worship
the Father in spirit and truth.*

JOHN 4:23

THE APEX OF OUR FELLOWSHIP and communion with the triune God is holy worship. Worship of God originates with God, not man. Worship was never the idea or plan of man, as there's nothing in us that seeks after God or even desires to know him (Rom. 3:11). The desire to worship God is wrought in the heart of believers by the Holy Spirit. We love God because he first loved us. We seek God because he first sought us. We worship God because he commands such worship, and we willingly obey.

## Beautiful Worship

John Owen said that the church should regularly be finding ways to express worship in manners that are "more decent, beautiful, and orderly."[1] What did Owen mean by "beautiful" worship? For worship to be biblically beautiful, Owen believed, it must focus on the triune God.

> All acceptable devotion in them that worship God is the effect of faith, which respects the precepts and promises of God alone. And the comeliness and beauty of gospel worship consisteth in its relation unto God by Jesus Christ, as the merciful high priest over his house, with the glorious administration of the Spirit therein.[2]

We would do well to keep in mind that "God is spirit, and those who worship him must worship in spirit and truth" (John 4:24). This is the only manner of devotion and worship that God accepts. God seeks those who will worship "in spirit." The text does not say "in *the* Spirit" but "in spirit." Jesus is not instructing believers to worship in the Holy Spirit but *with* or *in* the human spirit. He is telling the Samaritan woman in John 4 not only that he desires worship that flows from a knowledge of the truth of who he is, but also that he is looking for worshipers who will worship from the very depth of their inner being—their spirit.

Authentic biblical worship occurs only when the very core of our being is employed in worshiping God. Our lips may mouth the words, our hands may be lifted upward, our eyes may fill with tears, but unless these expressions flow from "the effect of faith," as Owen describes, our worship is mere performance. Valid worship proceeds from the heart of faith, for "without faith it is impossible to please him, for whoever would draw near to God must believe that he exists and that he rewards those who seek him" (Heb. 11:6). Worship isn't born in the void of our conscience but proceeds from truth. The truth of who God is as revealed in his word, the understanding of who Christ is and what he accomplished in his incarnation, the realization of who the Spirit is and what he is currently doing in our lives. Without truth born in faith, worship becomes ordinary, humdrum, and even carnal.

### Gospel Simplicity

Gospel-shaped worship is beautiful when it flows from a mind informed by truth and a heart willing to abandon all for the sake of communion with God. The gospel simplicity that replaces ceremonialist performance is the message of salvation through faith in God's final Word to man—Jesus Christ. He is infinitely more beautiful than gold or jewels. Christ's sacrificial death on the cross has obtained "an eternal redemption" for his people

(Heb. 9:12), making him "the mediator of a new covenant" (Heb. 9:15). Before, there was trepidation; now there is boldness. Before, there was slavery; now there is liberty. Before, there was complexity; now there is simplicity.

Worshipers are now free to come before the throne of grace, bypassing the folderol of the old way, now having access to a better way, for we "are no longer strangers and aliens, but you are now fellow citizens with the saints and members of the household of God" (Eph. 2:18–19).

The beauty of gospel worship, the worship with which we must concern ourselves as the bride of Christ, is found not in ritual and ceremony but in Christ and Christ alone. There is no glory in any other worship than the worship that comes by and is exclusively in Jesus Christ. For in him, the beauty of worship consists and becomes simple, spiritual, and heavenly.

# Shepherding the Flock

*Shepherd the flock of God that is among you.*

I PETER 5:2

FAITHFUL LEADERS BEAUTIFY THE CHURCH when they recognize that they are mere representatives of Christ and subordinate to him in all things. In other words, any authority these governing servants possess is a delegated authority from their sovereign head. When Jesus commissioned and sent out his disciples, he said, "All authority in heaven and on earth has been given to *me*. . . . And behold, *I am* with you always, to the end of the age" (Matt. 28:18, 20). Any authority leaders within the church retain is Christ's authority. That vicarious authority promises that he will be with us, working in and through us to exercise such jurisdiction in the love and care of his bride.

When leaders within the church admit and demonstrate that they are subservient to Christ, all other ministries within the church display a rare beauty that shines with the glory of Christ. In short, the church isn't a man-centered, egotistical spectacle but is a Christ-exalting organism led by gospel-driven servant-hood. All who desire to make the church beautiful adopt as their life motto "Not from men nor through man, but through Jesus Christ" (Gal. 1:1).

## The Ministry of a Pastor

Scripture is clear that the primary position of leadership and care within the body of Christ is the position of pastor. This office is known by many titles used interchangeably throughout the New Testament, such as *elder*, *bishop* or *overseer*, *shepherd* or *pastor*, *preacher*, and *teacher*.

It's evident that a pastor's role is singularly bound up with the varied duties of elder, overseer, shepherd, preacher, and teacher, all of which serve to care for, guide, instruct, and watch over the flock of God. To serve in this role or office, one must meet a high standard. Each man of God needs to endure a time of testing or proving to be placed in such a lofty position of shepherding oversight (1 Tim. 3:2–3).

A church radiates the beauty of Christ only when they are faithful to appoint men who themselves are beautiful in character and holiness. We all have heard and read devastating stories of churches that lose all credibility and destroy their witness because they appoint men to leadership positions who fail to meet those qualifications. That is not to say that churches must find perfect men to serve. There are no sinless leaders. Instead, the church needs to find men who, through proper testing and refining, demonstrate that they meet the biblical injunction and qualifications to serve.

To be a biblically faithful pastor and faithfully beautify the church, one's heart must beat in rhythm with the heart of Christ, both privately and publicly. There is no room for error in doctrine or failure in holiness.

## The Ministry of a Deacon

In addition to the office of pastor another critical role within the life of the body is that of a deacon. While Scripture doesn't specifically detail a deacon's responsibilities within the church, it does emphasize the key qualification for such an office—moral character. The attention Scripture devotes to the moral integrity, spiritual maturity, and doctrinal purity of those who serve the body of Christ highlights the importance of holiness within the life of the church and how such holiness serves to beautify.

49

A deacon is a servant. Originally, the verb *diakoneō* may have meant "serve tables" (Acts 6:2). But more broadly, the noun *diakonos* came to represent those who give themselves to any service to meet the needs of the people. A deacon is, like the governing authorities, a "servant for your good" and a "servant of God" (Rom. 13:3–4).

If we were to sum up a deacon's qualifications in a single phrase, it would be "full of the Spirit" (Acts 6:3; cf. Eph. 5:18). A deacon's moral character must be above reproach in all things. In public, deacons must prove exemplary in life, speech, integrity, and heart. In private, deacons must also evidence commitment to the truth of God's word and the holiness of their homes.

A deacon beautifies the church, first, by being a visible, unassuming, unadorned representative of the Lord Jesus Christ. Second, the deacon is a selfless servant to all. He doesn't pick and choose his favorite people to help. He willingly and sacrificially sets his desires aside to serve the widow, the hungry, the poor, the grieving, the helpless, and the sick alike. Third, the deacon helps "bring justice to the fatherless" and pleads "the widow's cause" (Isa. 1:17). He helps beautify the church by caring for those who have no one else to care for them.

Christ, the supreme head of the church, doesn't leave us to grope about in darkness, trying to discover innovative ways to lead and help ourselves. He's dispensed all we need and administers his bride's authority, leadership, and care by assigning specific biblical offices to be his representatives on earth.

9

# Feeding the Flock

*Preach the word.*

2 TIMOTHY 4:2

IN 2 TIMOTHY 4, with sweeping brushstrokes, Paul paints a beautiful picture of an undershepherd.

## Pastoral Charge

After a series of exhortations to Timothy, Paul begins one final injunction by imploring Timothy, "I charge you . . ." (2 Tim. 4:1). In Greek, this phrase is not composed of three words like our English translation but is one strong word that expresses an earnest testimony, solemn command, and strong urging. Paul isn't offering suggestions here but is voicing a strong compulsion for fervent ministry faithfulness. He, in effect, escorts Timothy into an ancient courtroom and says, "The full case of the entirety of your ministry, Timothy, will be drawn up against you in the court of God, where Christ Jesus is the Judge."

This is a summons for every man of God who has been called to the lofty yet humbling task of proclaiming the unsearchable riches of Christ—to stand in the eternal courtroom of God's presence. The pastor will not have a team of lawyers to argue his case or witnesses to testify of his good works. Still, the whole of his ministry—every sermon preached, every prayer prayed, every deed performed—will be open before the examining, flaming eyes of Christ (Rev. 19:12).

This isn't meant to frighten those contemplating a call to ministry, or seminarians preparing to enter the church, or even those who have been fulfilling their pastoral charge for decades. This charge reminds us of the seriousness with which we must view the calling of being the representatives of Christ in the world. Ministry isn't a quick way to make a buck. The church isn't a fast track to renown or notoriety.

God elevates the call to serve the church to a level of eternal scrutiny, warning us to think twice before beginning the journey: "Not many of you should become teachers, my brothers, for you know that we who teach will be judged with greater strictness" (James 3:1). All ministry is to be carried out with constant mindfulness that everything we do is under the watchful eye of God. Therefore, no argument is sustainable for a lackadaisical attitude of wasting time on frivolous things at the expense of tending the flock of God.

## "Preach the Word"

Paul distills the pastor's paramount task to a single phrase: "Preach the word" (2 Tim. 4:2). Such a simple statement, yet the pulse of every undershepherd of Christ. A preacher is to herald the word! The word translated "preach" is the Greek verb meaning "herald, proclaim, and announce publicly." During the Roman Empire, the word was often associated with those sent from the emperor's imperial court to publicly deliver a message to the people.

What is it we herald?

Paul designates the object of our message as "the word" (2 Tim. 4:2). That is, "all Scripture" (2 Tim. 3:16). Paul's sermons were not filled with intellectual platitudes of man's seeming superior wisdom. He wrote, "I, when I came to you, brothers, did not come proclaiming to you the testimony of God with lofty speech or wisdom" (1 Cor. 2:1). Lest anyone think gospel heralds have a message of mere interpretive opinion or suggestion, we're reminded that "what we proclaim is not ourselves, but Jesus Christ as Lord" (2 Cor. 4:5). Nothing should stand as a dam between the refreshing truth of God and the arid lands of the human heart. Only the unceasing proclamation of Christ is sufficient to quench such longing thirst.

How often are we to proclaim the word? "In season and out of season" (2 Tim. 4:2).

Pastors are to broadcast every jot and tittle of God's word when the message is *in* and when the message is *out*. When those around you are interested and when they aren't interested. When the message is popular and when it's not popular. The whims of the people must never determine the frequency and substance of preaching. Regardless of the popularity of the message, the pastor is to be ready "in season and out of season" to "reprove, rebuke, and exhort" (2 Tim. 4:2). As with a military guard or a watchman on a tower warning of impending danger to the city, there's no off-season for the pastor. There is only absolute fearlessness.

Feeding the flock of God is a fundamental duty in contributing to the beauty and loveliness of the church. As God's truth is proclaimed, men and women are saved and sanctified, and the church is made beautiful.

10

# Good News

*How beautiful upon the mountains*
*are the feet of him who brings good news.*

ISAIAH 52:7

THE NEW TESTAMENT is unmistakably clear that God has called his church to be the principal agency for heralding the gospel of Christ. The believers in the church of Acts were zealous and passionate proclaimers of the good news of Jesus Christ. Peter's enemies told him and the other apostles, "You have filled Jerusalem with your teaching" (Acts 5:28). In response to their evangelistic efforts, Paul and his fellow missionaries were accused of turning the world upside down (Acts 17:6). As a result, "the Lord added to their number day by day those who were being saved" (Acts 2:47).

## The Gospel of God

Paul's introduction to his letter to the church in Rome makes it quite apparent that the entire epistle's theme is the good news of "the gospel of God" (Rom. 1:1). This good news of the gospel is

- "the good news of the kingdom of God" (Luke 16:16),
- "good news . . . of Jesus Christ" (Acts 8:12),
- "good news of peace" (Acts 10:36),
- "the gospel of the grace of God" (Acts 20:24),
- "the gospel of his Son" (Rom. 1:9),
- "the gospel of your salvation" (Eph. 1:13),
- "the gospel of the glory of the blessed God" (1 Tim. 1:11).

Surrounded by *bad* news at every turn, the church has been entrusted with *good* news, the good news of the gospel, which finds its foundation in God himself. The gospel is not an earthly message but a heavenly message. Paul says that this is the "gospel *of God*" (Rom. 1:1). The gospel is *about* God—his holiness, love, grace, wrath, and righteousness. But Paul's main emphasis here is that the gospel is *from* God. He is the single author and architect of the gospel. The gospel doesn't originate in the church. The church didn't invent the gospel. The gospel is a message given to the bride of Christ announcing his mediatorial triumph over sin, death, and the world.

The word translated "gospel" is a compound in Greek, *euangelion*. The prefix *eu* means "good." The primary root word *angelion* means "messenger" or "message." When those two words are placed together, the word *gospel* simply means "good news." The gospel is the good news of salvation through God's Son, Jesus Christ.

What is the message of God's beautiful gospel?

God sent his Son, the second person of the Trinity, the Lord Jesus Christ, to rescue sinners. He was born of a virgin and lived a sinlessly perfect and obedient life under the law. He was crucified on a cross as a substitute to pay the penalty of God's wrath against the sins of all those who would ever believe. In his body, he bore on that tree the punishment due to sinners and his perfect righteousness was imputed to them, making them acceptable in the sight of God. He was buried in a borrowed tomb and on the third day rose from the dead. He ascended back to the authority and power of the right hand of his Father to intercede for all believers. Now, everyone who by faith "calls on the name of the Lord will be saved" (Rom. 10:13). This isn't only good news; it's beautifully good news.

No church has the freedom to tamper with, tweak, add to, or subtract from the good news of Jesus Christ—we are just to herald it. For there is nothing more beautiful and lovely in the sight of God than the extricating of sinners from the kingdom of darkness and delivering them to the kingdom of light.

## Gospel Zeal

The impetus for our gospel zeal is the promise that

> all the ends of the earth shall see
>> the salvation of our God. (Isa. 52:10)

All evangelistic and missionary endeavors are fueled by the confidence that Christ is enthroned as the head of the church and has promised to ransom men and women from "every tribe and language and people and nation" (Rev. 5:8–9). This assurance fueled John Calvin to write to the king when evangelistic efforts were harshly suppressed in his homeland of France:

> Indeed, we are quite aware of what . . . lowly little men we are. . . . But our doctrine must tower unvanquished above all the glory and above all the might of the world, for it is not of us, but of the living God and his Christ whom the Father has appointed to "rule from sea to sea, and from the rivers even to the ends of the earth" (Ps. 72:8).[1]

"It is not of us," Calvin wrote. There's such a God-centeredness to the gospel that we cannot claim it as our own. It didn't originate with the church, for we merely "have this treasure in jars of clay, to show that the surpassing power belongs to God and not to us" (2 Cor. 4:7). The gospel is God's gospel, and we are called to proclaim it with all our might.

# 11

# In Remembrance

*Do this in remembrance of me.*

I CORINTHIANS 11:24

THE ORDINANCES OF BAPTISM and the Lord's Supper are two specific ways in which God accomplishes his beautifying work within his church. Some traditions call these two mandates sacraments to denote that they are *holy* things and should therefore be kept holy by the church. Regardless of what they are labeled, these two ordinances are taught in Scripture and are reserved by God to be practiced exclusively by the church.

## Baptism

Baptism is an act of obedience in a new life of faith and is not a suggested practice but a clear command, for discipleship is not complete without baptism.

Baptism is beautifully associated with repentance and faith. In Matthew 3, multitudes come to John the Baptist to be baptized as a symbol of their repentance from sin and turning to God (Matt. 3:6). Baptism is a symbol that points to saving faith; it is not the conveyer of saving grace (Eph. 2:8–9). Biblical baptism signifies a turning away from sin, a full-fledged embrace of Christ, and a believer's willingness to identify with him in his death, burial, and resurrection so that we can now "walk in newness of life" (Rom. 6:4).

Baptism beautifies the church in several ways. First, it exalts Christ by being a visible expression and reminder of his death, burial, and resurrection. Second, it energizes onlookers to obey Christ by making their own public confession of faith. Third, baptism announces the gospel. Apart from the gospel's proclamation in preaching, baptism is the most visual portrayal of the gospel possessed by the church. Fourth, baptism serves as a sign and a warning—a sign that forgiveness is available to all who place their faith in Christ, and a warning that unless you repent, "you will all likewise perish" (Luke 13:3).

As God's gift to his church, baptism is how he incorporates us into his fold, strengthens his body, beautifies his church, and draws more to himself.

## The Lord's Supper

Paul recalls the meal the Lord Jesus celebrated with his disciples the night before his death (Luke 22:14–23; 1 Cor. 11:23–26). Originally the meal of Passover, this old covenant feast was transformed by Jesus into a meal of infinitely greater significance. Rather than looking back to deliverance from Egypt, the Lord's Supper causes believers to reflect back to when their sins were atoned for by God's spotless Lamb while also looking forward to the great marriage supper of the Lamb, when we shall bask together in the resplendent glory of our Father.

The simple symbolic elements of bread and the cup—Christ's flesh and blood—become a beautifying influence upon the church as the supper demonstrates our remembering, loving, and examining.

*Remembering.* The supper becomes a path to congregational beauty as we come together to remember Christ. We need look no further than to the Lord's Supper to see Jesus, for through this celebratory meal, he has left us a portrait of himself to remember him. The very elements point to Christ. Without diving into the varied views, we may say that the bread represents his incarnate sinless flesh nailed to the cross, and the cup signifies the blood that poured forth for the atonement of sin. When eaten and drunk amid corporate worship, these elements together become one of the most explicit pictures of Jesus that the church retains.

*Loving.* The very symbols present within the meal highlight the selfless, sacrificial love poured forth by Christ on the cross. The Lord's Table is one of the foremost places within the church to gather in mutual love and reconciliation. This is why the Lord's Supper is not to be celebrated alone, for it is a congregational meal to demonstrate and foster genuine love among the people of God. At the table, we're reminded that the church is one, and our mutual love radiates forth to display a beautiful bride before a watching world.

*Examining.* For this type of mutual love and reconciliation to be present, each of us must examine himself or herself (1 Cor. 11:27–28). By examining ourselves, we perform a mental and internal survey of our relationship with Christ, our relationships with others, and our private and public sins. Now, the Lord's Supper isn't for the sinless—for no one is without sin—but is for those who have thoroughly examined every aspect of their lives, so far as is possible, and confessed and repented of sin with a wholehearted desire to walk with Christ.

While baptism identifies us with the death, burial, and resurrection of our Lord and the testimony of faith wrought within our hearts, the Lord's Supper is the frequent reminder that believers must remember the Lord, love one another, and continually deal with their sin. In these ways, both baptism and the Lord's Supper are visible ordinances whereby the Holy Spirit sanctifies believers. Through our participation in both, the Lord has provided a way in which his bride is inseparably linked to his cross and resurrection as the ultimate glory of her beauty.

## 12

# Walking Worthy

*Walk in a manner worthy of the calling*
*to which you have been called.*

EPHESIANS 4:1

PAUL SPENDS THE FIRST three chapters of his letter to the
Ephesian church assembling a doctrinal framework upon which
he will hang principles of right behavior. Paul never offers the
*how* without first giving us the *why*. These first three chapters of
Ephesians are the *why*—who we are in Christ. Paul then shifts
his discussion in chapter 4 to how believers are to live.

"I therefore" (v. 1) is an intentional shift from the theological
to the practical—*how* God's people should live as a result of *who*
they are. This whole applicatory section of Ephesians 4:1–6:20

is built upon the firm bedrock of Christ as the cornerstone of his church and the Spirit who empowers such living (Eph. 3:16).

## Walking in Christ

"I . . . urge you to walk" (Eph. 4:1). The metaphor of *walking* appears throughout Paul's letters and is always connected with an urgency in the Christian life. Paul understands this urgency. The admonitions Paul offers are dispensed not as suggestions or good ideas but as unequivocal commands for faithfulness in *being* and *living as* the body of Christ. This is your obedience in the gospel—you who once *walked* in transgressions and sins (Eph. 2:1–2)—you now must *walk* in the good works God has intended for you (Eph. 2:10).

Throughout the New Testament, the verb "walk" is a present tense Greek word referring to a continuous mode of conduct. The infinitive "to walk" can be rendered "to live." In his instructions to the church, Paul uses "walk" in this way to guarantee that they comprehend what correct Christian living is and what it is not. For Paul, "walking" is shorthand for practical Christian living—living out what has been planted within.

Other New Testament writers also employ the same image of walking to define the life of a believer. For instance, John says Christians are not to "walk in darkness" (1 John 1:6; 2:11). Believers should not continue to live in the sin from which they were rescued. In his Gospel record, John taught that Jesus was the true light for a sin-darkened world (John 1:4–5), and no one can rightly claim to be a true believer and follower of Christ who continues to walk in sinful darkness.

## Walking in the Light

In contrast to the darkness of the world, the bride of Christ is to "walk in the light" (1 John 1:7). Those who walk in the light do so because the Spirit of God has regenerated them and given them new life in Christ. When church members' feet are firmly fixed on the path of light, their lives will reflect the glory and majesty of the one who is the light. Your daily actions, attitudes, conversations, thoughts, and works will reflect a light-filled Christlikeness. Walking in the light results in a godly attitude so that, instead of lashing out at difficult people or becoming angry with those who disagree, you're actually brought into "fellowship with one another" (1 John 1:7).

As a result of walking in the light, the body of Christ also walks by the Spirit and therefore walks "worthy." At the precise moment of someone's salvation, the Holy Spirit begins to live within that person. Puritan Richard Sibbes believed that at the exact instant the Spirit takes up residence within us, he begins to knit our hearts to God and Jesus Christ. Sibbes explained, "The Spirit is the bond of union between Christ and us, and between God and us."[1] The role of the Spirit is to intimately acquaint us with the Father and the Son. He establishes communion between us and empowers us to walk. When the Spirit is present, he transforms our lives from one degree of glory to another. As he molds us into the image of Christ, the Spirit collectively empowers the church to walk in a Christlike manner.

While it is the Spirit who unleashes the dynamic power to walk in the Christian life, it is the individual Christian who must put one foot in front of the other. The Spirit fills every true believer within the household of faith, but those individual believers must work, teach, pray, and worship, propelling the church into a closer walk and joy in Jesus. The Spirit doesn't work for us, preach for us, evangelize for us, or even worship for us. He empowers his people to do all these things, but it is their responsibility to walk.

A church that is beautiful in the eyes of her bridegroom is a church that is walking "in a manner worthy of the calling to which you have been called" (Eph. 4:1). It is living lives that regularly confess sin and preeminently desire to walk according to the Spirit and not according to the flesh. Living lives that reflect their Master and image him forth to a watching world. Living lives that yearn to know him and have his gospel power flow in them for his good pleasure. Living lives that mutually display to all who see that the church is genuinely walking worthy.

13

# Blessed Persecution

*All who desire to live a godly life in*
*Christ Jesus will be persecuted.*

2 TIMOTHY 3:12

IN *FOXE'S BOOK OF MARTYRS*, we read the account of Protestant Reformer John Hooper, who was arrested and imprisoned when Mary I (eventually known as Bloody Mary) ascended the throne and immediately began to usher England back to Roman Catholicism. On numerous occasions, Hooper was ushered before assembled councils and commanded to recant his "Protestant heresy." Every time, he refused.

On February 9, 1555, Bishop Hooper was led to his place of execution in Gloucester, tied to a stake, and burned. When he reached the erected place of his death, an iron hoop was placed around his chest to secure him to the wooden stake. As the kindling was placed around him, he caught two bundles in his hands, kissed them, and put them under his arms. On that cold morning the blustery English wind was so fierce that the flames barely touched him. The bottom half of his body began to burn, but only slightly, while the fire never reached his upper body, except his hair. Hopper cried: "Lord Jesus, have mercy upon me! Lord Jesus, have mercy upon me! Lord Jesus, receive my spirit!" These were his final words that emerged from the flames. Little by little he burned. First one finger, then the next. One arm fell off into the fire, and then the next, until finally he yielded up his spirit.

Paul warned Timothy, "All who desire to live a godly life in Christ Jesus will be persecuted" (2 Tim. 3:12). Paul was deeply persuaded that conflict is inevitable between the church composed of those living righteously and those in the world who revel in their ungodliness. There is an undeniable tension between light and darkness.

Lest we think the church is immune to or exempt from persecutions and sufferings in our modern age, Jesus reminds us, "The world hates you" (John 15:18).

## Reasons for Persecution

In the conclusion of his Beatitude statements in Matthew 5, Jesus pronounces a divine blessing upon those who suffer persecution.[1] Why will his hearers face persecution? Because they exhibit the godly characteristics of the previous beatitudes. Jesus defines persecution and suffering arising from two sources.

First, true disciples of Christ are persecuted "for righteousness" (Matt. 5:10). The type of righteousness on display in the beatitudes—humility, meekness, peacemaking, hunger for righteousness—will inevitably elicit persecution from the world. The ungodly witness the church's righteousness and see such holiness as a condemnation of their unrighteous behavior. In response, they lash out in ridicule and malign the church through severe forms of persecution and suffering.

Second, true disciples of Christ are persecuted "on my [Jesus's] account," or as several translations put it, "because of me [Jesus]" (Matt. 5:11). He highlights a particular *name*— a Christological title—that, when we are identified with it, causes persecution and ridicule. According to Luke 6:22, many will instigate particular hostility against unbelievers "on account of the Son of Man." This specific title identifies Jesus as a King of divine, heavenly origin, who will reign over a universal and eternal kingdom and is worthy of worship by all peoples of the earth. When the church identifies with the Christ of the Bible—divine ruler of the cosmos, worthy of all worship—she exhibits an alien righteousness that is unique in character. This righteousness is not of her own making or invention. This distinctive, heavenly righteousness has been gifted to her by Christ on the cross, who desired to beautify his bride by granting her an unparalleled message: Jesus is King.

## Expressions of Persecution

Jesus says in Matthew 5:11 that others will "revile you." Reviling is the picture of someone mocking and verbally shaming you, pronouncing over you humiliating and discrediting words.

Second, the word "persecute" in verse 11 means "run after, pursue, or run out." Jesus is warning his disciples that they may be sought from town to town by those driven by evil intentions, may endure violent abuse, and may even be turned over to the authorities.

Third, verse 11 states that adversaries will "utter all kinds of evil against you falsely on my account." The persecutors of Jesus's followers will raise allegations against them that have no basis in reality but are lies.

There is no substance to deceitful lies, false accusations, and mockery invented to persecute those within the church. A church devoted to righteousness, godliness, and the gospel of Christ will be persecuted and reviled because that same righteousness, godliness, and gospel come as an indictment against the sinful lifestyle of unbelievers.

## Rejoice and Be Glad!

If we were only given Matthew 5:11, we might despair. But Jesus gives us more: "Rejoice and be glad, for your reward is great in heaven, for so they persecuted the prophets who were before you" (Matt. 5:12). Rejoice while suffering? Be glad amid ridicule? How can this be? This mystery is unveiled in the depth of our unyielding assurance that being with Jesus in glory will far more than reward us for any suffering we have faced in this life.

To "be glad" is to enjoy a state of utter happiness and well-being. "Rejoice" is similar in meaning to being glad but is more intense. This denotes extreme gladness and extreme joy.

The forward-looking faith of Moses is an example to us all: "He considered the reproach of Christ greater wealth than the treasures of Egypt, for he was looking to the reward" (Heb. 11:26).

14

# We Are One

*There is one body.*

EPHESIANS 4:4

ONENESS AMONG THE PEOPLE of God is a defining characteristic of the church. We don't have to read far into the New Testament until we find Jesus speaking of the oneness of his bride. The content of his high priestly prayer in John 17 abounds with oneness petitions. Without this unity, the world is likely to see the church as a human organization devised by creative ingenuity, not a body of divine origin. Discord plagues man-made institutions—love, peace, harmony, community, and fellowship eventually break down. Jesus is praying that when the world views the church, it will see not a man-made organization

79

but a divine organism born from God. The church's growing *oneness* is what defines the church as having an *otherness*.

Since unity of the faith is indispensable to the church's ministries, her knowledge of Christ, her maturity in the faith, and her imaging of God to the world, we must consider it a command and duty to preserve and perfect this unity within the church. What are some practical ways individual believers can foster a true unity that manifests itself within the one body?

## Unity Requires One-Anothering

There are fifty-nine "one another" statements in the New Testament that speak directly to what we are to do and how we are to act toward each other. For example:

- "Be at peace with one another" (Mark 9:50).
- "Love one another" (John 13:34).
- "Serve one another" (Gal. 5:13).
- "Forgiving one another" (Eph. 4:32).
- "Admonishing one another" (Col. 3:16).
- "Encourage one another" (1 Thess. 4:18).
- "Do not speak evil against one another" (James 4:11).
- "Show hospitality to one another" (1 Pet. 4:9).

As these samples show, the "one another" statements divert attention from ourselves to others. Others become the focus of our ministry.

The "one another" passages are not suggestions for a successful life but commands for right Christian living. Unity is impossible when we consider ourselves more significant than others. The anthem of disunity is "me, myself, and I." We desire our opinions to be heard, our views considered, and our plans fulfilled. We could go as far as to say that unity requires the obliteration of self. It is the complete denial of self to maintain love, fellowship, and peace within the church. By obeying these injunctions, believers ultimately obey the second great commandment, to love one's neighbor as oneself (Mark 12:31), which puts the gospel of Christ on display as the transformative power it claims to possess. Have you wondered how you can beautify the bride of Christ? "One another" fellow believers.

### Unity Requires Sanctified Truthfulness

True unity in the church exists only where her members declare with one harmonious voice, "Your word is truth" (John 17:17). Based on the inerrant and sufficient word of God, sound doctrine is essential in fostering true unity. In John 17, Jesus prays that his people would be sanctified in the truth (v. 17). "Sanctify" means "make holy." It involves setting something or someone apart from sin. Jesus says that God's word contains the proper ingredients for holiness: "Your word is truth." Therefore, since Scripture is the means whereby believers are made holy, our churches mustn't be a smorgasbord of varied beliefs and ideas, but must be an exquisitely set table offering the scriptural nourishment that causes growth into the image of Christ. If a church is seemingly unified without sound theology, her unity resides in amusing sentimentality or overt falsehood. True unity consists of sanctified truthfulness that bases every ministry, sermon, and decision upon the word of God.

## Unity Requires Gospel Fidelity

As we have already explored, any church that doesn't have a biblical understanding of the gospel cannot be called a true church. The key here is not only the gospel in the evangelistic terms of justifying, forgiving, and saving, but also the gospel in terms of sanctifying, growing, and maturing as Christians. Unity within the church is a wholehearted commitment to gospel fidelity within her people's everyday lives. From how we teach children to how we train for ministry, we must be committed to the faithfulness, dependability, and transformative effects of the gospel to have lasting results. The gospel unifies the very culture of the church. If for one moment we imagine that our creativity, entrepreneurship, initiative, or even intellect is the impetus by which Christians grow in Christ, we will be fractured. Authentic unity is fostered by a

daily awareness of our need for the life, death, burial, resurrection, and ascension of Jesus.

———

Unity is critical because it fosters maturity, doctrinal stability,
discernment, a loving vocabulary, Christlike growth, church-
wide equipping, and spiritual building. Our oneness reflects
Christ, who beams forth his glory in every sphere of the church
to make her increasingly beautiful. May our prayer echo the
words of Charles Spurgeon: "Bless this our beloved church: keep
them still in unity and earnestness of heart. In all fresh advances
that we hope to make, be with us and help us."[1]

# Epilogue

*The king has brought me into his chambers.*
SONG OF SOLOMON 1:4

A KING'S INNER CHAMBERS are the most secluded, private, and heavily guarded rooms within his palace. Here, his bride is welcomed as his peculiar treasure and joy.

This book has essentially served as a visit to the sacred chambers where Christ dwells alone with his church. We have been led into the inner workings of the triune God as he rescues and sanctifies a people and makes them fit for his glory. Here, we are called his friends, his bride, his possession, his children, his house. Here, we can call him our Father, our Friend, our Savior, our Head, our Helper, and our Beautifier. Within these chambers, the church is robed in beauty, arrayed in loveliness, and set upon a path of lifelong adoration, intimate fellowship, selfless service, and gospel proclamation.

The church isn't just about organization, leadership, function, and vision. There's something much more beautiful and lovely to recognize. The church is about people being rescued, redeemed, and renewed. The church is about savoring, rejoicing, and service. The church is about proclaiming, enduring, and walking. The church is about *being* the bride adorned, beautiful, and lovely.

Though we visit these chambers often, one day our king will invite us into his chambers forever. That celebration will be inaugurated with the marriage supper of the Lamb. On this day, the bridegroom will consummate all things, and we shall be arrayed in garments white as snow as we enter eternal, unbroken fellowship with the Father, Son, and Holy Spirit.

This book was meant for people who find themselves in a million different places, scattered abroad in local churches in every continent of the world, faithfully plodding, praying for a renewed hope and glimpse of the beauty and loveliness of the church.

The King has thrown open the doors.

He welcomes you to enter.

He bids you to gaze upon his bride and proclaim, "Behold, you are beautiful!" (Song 1:15).

# Notes

*Introduction*

1. Jonathan Edwards, "The Church's Marriage to Her Sons, and to Her God," in *Sermons and Discourses, 1743–1758*, ed. Wilson H. Kimnach, vol. 25 of *The Works of Jonathan Edwards* (New Haven, CT: Yale University Press, 2006), 187.

2. Jonathan Edwards, *Writings on the Trinity, Grace, and Faith*, ed. Sang Hyun Lee, vol. 21 of *The Works of Jonathan Edwards* (New Haven, CT: Yale University Press, 2003), 142.

*Chapter 1: You Are Beautiful*

1. John Gill, *An Exposition of the Book of Solomon's Song* (London: William Hill Collingridge, 1854), 57.

2. Jonathan Edwards, "Miscellanies," 271, in *The Miscellanies, Entry Nos. a–z, aa–zz, 1–500*, ed. Thomas A. Schafer, vol. 13 of *The Works of Jonathan Edwards* (New Haven, CT: Yale University Press, 1994), 374.

*Chapter 2: The Household of God*

1. John Owen, *The Works of John Owen*, ed. William H. Goold, 24 vols. (1850–1855; repr., vols. 1–16, Edinburgh: Banner of Truth,

1965–1968), 1:485. See also Sinclair Ferguson, *John Owen on the Christian Life* (Edinburgh: Banner of Truth, 1987), 158.

2. Ferguson, *John Owen*, 159.

*Chapter 7: In Spirit and Truth*

1. John Owen, *Brief Instruction*, in *The Works of John Owen*, ed. William H. Goold, 24 vols. (1850–1855; repr., vols. 1–16, Edinburgh: Banner of Truth, 1965–1968), 15:467. See Joel R. Beeke and Mark Jones, "John Owen on the Christian Sabbath and Worship," chap. 41 in *A Puritan Theology* (Grand Rapids, MI: Reformation Heritage, 2012), 653–79.

2. Owen, *Works*, 15:467.

*Chapter 10: Good News*

1. John Calvin, prefatory address to King Francis, in *Institutes of the Christian Religion*, ed. John T. McNeill, trans. Ford Lewis Battles (Philadelphia: Westminster Press, 1960), 13.

*Chapter 12: Walking Worthy*

1. Richard Sibbes, "A Description of Christ," in *The Complete Works of Richard Sibbes*, ed. Alexander B. Grosart, 7 vols. (1862–1864; repr., Edinburgh: Banner of Truth, 1978–1983), 1:17.

*Chapter 13: Blessed Persecution*

1. This chapter, particularly this section and the following, draws upon Dustin Benge, "The Persecution Driven Life," *reformation21*, August 31, 2018, https://www.reformation21.org/blogs/the-persecution -driven-life.php.

*Chapter 14: We Are One*

1. Charles H. Spurgeon, *The Pastor in Prayer* (London: Elliot Stock, 1893), 143.

# Scripture Index

# Union

**We fuel reformation in churches and lives.**

Union Publishing invests in the next generation of leaders with theology that gives them a taste for a deeper knowledge of God. From books to our free online content, we are committed to producing excellent resources that will refresh, transform, and grow believers and their churches.

We want people everywhere to know, love, and enjoy God, glorifying him in everything they do. For this reason, we've collected hundreds of free articles, podcasts, book chapters, and video content for our free online collection. We also produce a fresh stream of written, audio, and video resources to help you to be more fully alive in the truth, goodness, and beauty of Jesus.

If you are hungry for reformational resources that will help you delight in God and grow in Christ, we'd love for you to visit us at unionpublishing.org.

**unionpublishing.org**

# Union Series

**Full & Concise Editions**

*Rejoice and Tremble | What Does It Mean to Fear the Lord?*

*Deeper | How Does God Change Us?*

*The Loveliest Place | Why Should We Love the Local Church?*

The Union series invites readers to experience deeper enjoyment of God through four interconnected values: delighting in God, growing in Christ, serving the church, and blessing the world.

For more information, visit **crossway.org**.